MYCHAL WYN

On Parenting:

Ten Steps *to* Helping *your* Child Succeed *in* School

VOLUME I

MYCHAL WYNN

On Parenting:

Ten Steps *to* Helping *your* Child Succeed *in* School

VOLUME I

RISING SUN
PUBLISHING

Mychal Wynn On Parenting:
Ten Steps to Helping your Child Succeed in School
Volume I

THIRD EDITION 2006

ISBN 1-880463-50-4
Copyright © 1999 Mychal Wynn
Copyright © 1999 Rising Sun Publishing, Inc.

Special quantity discounts available for PTA/PTSA and community organizations.

Cover photograhs taken by Mychal Wynn.

P.O. Box 70906
Marietta, GA 30007-0906

770.518.0369/800.524.2813
FAX 770.587.0862
E-mail: info@rspublishing.com
Web site: http://www.rspublishing.com

Printed in the United States of America.

Acknowledgments

I would like to thank God, the ultimate comforter and counselor as I step and stumble through the challenges of being a husband to my wife and father to my children.

I would like to thank my editor, Denise Mitchell Smith, a wife and mother. Your thoughts and insight have been invaluable.

I would like to thank Linda Richardson, of the Baltimore County Schools, whose parent book club put the ideas contained within this book into practice.

Thanks also to the many parents who have reviewed my thoughts, shared their input, and given of their time to ensure that this book is practical and do-able for all parents.

Dedication

This book is dedicated to my wife, Nina, an extraordinary wife and mother.

To my sons, Mychal-David and Jalani, who, like the thousands of children I see in our schools each year, are born into the world with divinely-given gifts and extraordinary potential. Never give up on your dreams.

And, to my parents, who, without the benefit of all of the research and thoughts outlined in this book, did the best they could with all they had, to prepare me to follow my dreams. Thank you.

Contents

About the Author

Mychal and his wife, Nina, have two sons, Mychal-David (17) and Jalani (12). They have firsthand experience with the many challenges and frustrations facing parents. While Mychal is traveling around the country speaking to parents, teachers, and students, and Nina is busy running a publishing company, the telephone rings:

"Jalani hit a little girl and bit a little boy."

"Jalani would not go to sleep at nap time."

"Mychal-David would not stop talking in class."

"Jalani used bad words today."

"Mychal-David has not been turning in his work."

"Jalani would not be quiet at story time."

"Mychal-David broke the pencil sharper."

"Jalani kicked a hole in the wall."

"Jalani would not sit in time-out, so he was sent to the office and you have to come and get him right now!"

If responding to the frequent notes, meeting with teachers, counselors, and the principal, and dealing with their children's behaviors were not enough, Mychal and Nina must develop, revise, develop, and revise again strategies to get their older son to do his class work ("I am not motivated in class"), turn in his homework, and bring home the many notices that he receives from school.

*"When our older son, Mychal-David, graduated from the fifth grade, Nina and I celebrated. This day marked the end of another school year. For eight years, dating back to his preschool days at the First Lutheran Church in Carson, California, we have prayed for solutions, researched everything that we could find about parenting and teaching, developed and implemented strategies, and prayed again for the wisdom and strength to help our children develop their potential and to become successful in school. Today marked the end of elementary school and was **our** day of celebration!"*

Their older son is now in his final year of high school and has already been admitted into Amherst College. Mychal and Nina believe the strategies they have used with their children can be replicated by other parents. Countless children who are underachieving in school, and others who have been diagnosed as Hyperactive, Emotional/Behavioral Disorder (EBD), Learning Disabled (LD), or with Attention Deficit Disorder (ADD) have special talents and abilities that can be channeled into long-term dreams and aspirations. All children can succeed in school as they journey along the road to richly rewarding lives and careers.

Foreword

In Mychal Wynn's presentations to teachers, parents, and students, he brings a message of hope, of dreams, and of the potential and possibilities within each of our lives. This book is part of Mychal Wynn's school improvement/ student achievement series of books which outline parenting, teaching, and school reform strategies from preschool through high school. Each book is designed to provide ideas and strategies to help parents help their children achieve success in school, teachers achieve success in the classroom, administrators achieve success in creating high-performing schools, and students achieve success in their journey from preschool into postsecondary education.

Mychal Wynn has shared his strategies with parents and teachers throughout the United States, Canada, the U.S. Virgin Islands, and Bermuda—commonsense strategies which he and his wife have used with their own children. Throughout this book you will find examples of situations which he and his wife have experienced with their two sons. Although the situations and circumstances of your family might differ, the strategies outlined are appropriate for the complete spectrum of today's families: two-parent households, single parents, foster parents, grandparents, teen parents, and working parents. This book is designed for all parents, in all situations, experiencing all types of circumstances.

There is no single approach or perfect solution to all of the day-to-day challenges facing parents, however, we believe the ideas and strategies presented in each book in the series will help any parent, teacher, mentor, coach, or counselor in developing an effective game plan for increasing a child's success from preschool through high school.

Other books in the school improvement/ student achievement series:

- *Increasing Student Achievement: Volume I, Vision*
- *A Middle School Plan for Students with College-Bound Dreams*
- *A High School Plan for Students with College-Bound Dreams*
- *Follow Your Dreams: Lessons That I Learned in School*
- *The Eagles who Thought They were Chickens*
- *Empowering African-American Males: Teaching, Parenting, and Mentoring Successful Black Males*

Introduction

My wife and I have learned that successful parenting is holistic, meaning that we must develop strategies for each piece of the parenting puzzle. What we do with our sons at home to prepare them to succeed in school, how we work with their respective schools, how we establish a system of rewards and consequences, and how we communicate their needs to, and collaborate with their teachers, are all pieces of the parenting puzzle.

The focus of this book is on those things that we, as parents, can do to shape what happens to our children when they are in school and to prepare the foundation for long-term school success. The books, *A Middle School Plan for Students with College-Bound Dreams*, and *A High School Plan for Students with College-Bound Dreams* supplement the information provided in this book by focusing on specific strategies for the middle and high school years. However, a successful journey through the seven--year middle-high school continuum requires a solid preschool through elementary school foundation.

My wife and I have just gone through another school year; one of joy and pain, of hope and frustration, of teacher conferences, and administrator meetings. While our children are far from perfect, my wife and I are their advocates. The school cannot take total credit for their successes, nor can it place total blame for any failures onto their shoulders. What and how much they learn is as much a function of their learning styles as it is each of their teachers' teaching styles. How they behave in class is influenced by how my wife and I "teach" them to behave at home, coupled with how their classroom teacher "allows" them to behave at school.

This, and each book in the school improvement/student achievement series, has been written for anyone who wants to become a child's advocate. You cannot become a child's advocate without accepting ownership for influencing school change. The best students can still fail when attending low-performing schools just as average students can excel when attending high-performing schools.

While my wife and I work diligently to ensure that our children leave home with dreams and aspirations which inspires them to learn, we must work just as diligently with the teachers and staff in their respective schools to ensure that what happens in school does not destroy their dreams and aspirations once they get there.

We do not believe our children or any children should sit in classrooms for 180 days each year from kindergarten through the twelfth grade to just "get an education." We believe they must get the education which *best* prepares them to pursue their dreams and aspirations.

We also believe that schools should foster a school climate and culture which inspires within children a passion and purpose for coming to school. We do not want our sons to become one the thousands of children who shuffle through the day; whose eyes reveal lost and abandoned souls; who spend most of their time in school clowning, socializing, disrupting classrooms, bullying or being bullied by other children, or in other ways are distracted from or tuned out to learning.

Instead of chapters, this book sets forth ten steps. Each step is designed to provide questions that you should ask and things that you should do on your child's behalf to increase the possibilities of your child succeeding in his or her school. While you may prefer to read the book all the way through, I would suggest that you take each step one at a time, and, by all means, keep a journal or notebook. Make notes and highlight the strategies which you intend to immediately use. Gather your information slowly and over an extended period of time. Throughout the school year, as you gain more insight into your child, pass helpful information on to your child's teacher. Keep in mind that your child's best opportunity to succeed lies in your ability to develop a positive relationship and an effective partnership with your child's teacher.

As a result of the interest demonstrated by teachers, many of whom are parents themselves, this book has been updated to include teacher-specific strategies. These have been set forth in boxes labeled, "Teacher Strategies." If you are a parent you may want to make copies of these pages and pass them on to your child's teacher to further develop the necessary parent-teacher partnership to ensure your child's school success.

According to the African proverb, "It takes a village to raise a child." The ideas that follow provide ways of strengthening the village so that we may better enable our children to succeed.

Children We Care

Black, brown, red, yellow, and white
    children of all colors with eyes so bright
Given us in innocence, no burdens to bear
    how can we say to you, "Children we care?"
How can we convince you that the love we give
    is the most treasured possession of the life we live
Toys, gifts, and trips to the zoo
    are a very small part of the things that we do
We love, nurture, and guide you along
    laying the foundation from which to grow strong
We teach you, protect you, and always demand
    that in learning you simply do the best that you can
And often the expectations that we have of you
    are greater than you believe is the best you can do
It's because in our lives we continue to see
    that we rarely become the best we can be
Our love and our lives, we always will share
    forgive our mistakes, because "Children we care."

— Mychal Wynn

S tep 1

Get to Know Your Child

Getting to know your son or daughter is the first, and arguably, the most difficult step. As parents, we grew up in a different generation. We were taught different values than those constantly being directed at our children through today's music, movies, literature, and advertisements—not to mention the Internet. For many of us, family and church were the most important influences in our lives. For many of today's children, the influence of family is replaced by the powerful influences of peers and the media (i.e., television, radio, music, movies, videos, video games, and the Internet). The influence of church or spirituality in the lives of many children is no longer first or second, if on the list at all.

With parents operating from such a different belief system, coupled with the natural cross-gender (mothers to sons, fathers to daughters) and cross-generational (middle-age parents to young children) communication problems, most parents will admit "I do not understand my son at all!" You have probably said on more than one occasion, "I just do not understand that boy. He is so hard headed!"; or, "What is wrong with these girls today, they have no self respect"; or, "Thirteen-year-olds are just crazy!"; or, "We did not do things like that when I was a kid."

If we admittedly do not understand our sons or daughters it is not because we, as parents, are stupid, or that our children are insane (at least not all of the time). It is because we, as parents, were not taught how to understand our children. Our parents probably did not understand us. They simply told us what to do and expected us to do it. Remember your parents telling you to do something? You dared not question why. And besides, if you had, their answer would have been, "Because I said 'Do it'!" They did not know (and probably did not care) anything about our learning styles, the teachers' teaching styles, our personality types or anything else. They told us to go to school, pay attention, do what our teachers told us to do, and get a good education. We were to be seen and not heard. We were to sit still and be quiet.

Now we are parents. Most us do not want to do to our children what our parents did to us (which was not all bad, but it was not all good). However, we do not know what else to do. We were not taught how to become parents by our parents. We were not taught how to be parents in school, so, many of us are making it up as we go; and with today's influences on our children, we are drowning. Our ships are sinking, we are bailing water, and we need someone to throw us a rope!

> Multiple children, raised in the same home, by the same parents, with the same values are likely to grow into entirely different people. Which may cause you to question, "Is this really our child?"

Compounding all of this is that we simply do not understand our children. How could we? We "see" our children through our perceptions of ourselves and we "understand" our children only as well as we understand ourselves. But how well do we know ourselves? Of all the classes we have taken, of all the subjects we have studied, how many have helped us to better understand ourselves? Do you know what your personality type is? Do you know what your learning style is? Do you know the many ways in which you are smart or the many ways in which you can become smarter? How could you when you were told, "Sit still and be quiet"; when you were told, "Shut up and pay attention"; when you were told, "Children should be seen and not heard?"

Our first step is not only getting to know our children, but getting to know ourselves.

In our household we have made a conscious effort to better understand who we are and how each of us is different. It has helped our sons, two exact opposite personality types, to understand why they rarely want to do the same things. It has helped them to understand why certain things they say or do affects their mother one way and me another. And, it has helped my wife and me to teach our sons in the ways in which they best learn.

Understanding each other has reduced the conflicts in our household between our children, between ourselves and our children, and between my wife and me. Why we are different is far more than race, gender, values, and beliefs. While all of these are a part of our differences, how we learn, what our personalities are, and how we best express our unique gifts and abilities are all pieces to the puzzle of who we are.

It is natural for us to project our values, beliefs, personality, and ways of understanding things onto our children. However, by doing this we fail to "see" our children in their own uniqueness, with their own values, beliefs, personality, and ways of understanding things. While they are our children, they are not born with our values, beliefs, or sense of right and wrong. And, they certainly may not have our personality or understand things in the ways in which we do. While we may teach and cultivate our values and beliefs, our children's personality and the ways in which they understand things is uniquely theirs. As parents, we must learn *how* to best help our children *learn* the values and develop the character we want them to have. To successfully teach our children, we must better understand the uniqueness of their personality and the ways in which they best learn.

Hello ... Is anybody home?

Our then, seven-year-old, son, Jalani, often said, "Ding, dong, ding, dong. Hello, is anybody home?" Have you ever wondered, "Is anybody home?" when talking to your children?

Perhaps the most frustrating part of parenting is that oftentimes we talk and talk and talk, and our children just do not get it! Which of the following statements have you used in the past?

"I do not know what is wrong with this boy."

"She never does what I tell her to do!"

"Did you understand what I told you?"

"Why do you keep doing that when we have already discussed it?"

"Why do you keep asking me? I have already told you, 'No.' "

"What is wrong with you? You know that you can do better."

"I do not understand why you keep getting low grades in math; I never had problems with math."

"What is wrong with you? Did you *hear* what I *said*?"

"I am tired of telling you to do the same thing over and over."

"If I have to *tell* you one more time ..."

"You are wearing on my last nerve!"

"Why did you do that? You know better. If I have told you once, I have told you a thousand times."

"Have you lost your mind?"

Even after our parenting cup runneth over, there is no end to the many seemingly insane things that children do. Bill Cosby, in his wonderful monologue on parenting, attributes our children's insanity to their having brain damage!

Despite our children's apparent insanity (or brain damage), we, as parents, make two critical mistakes in our efforts to understand our children.

Mistake #1

We project our childhood experiences onto our children to reason, rationalize, or explain their behaviors.

"No matter what my friends did, I knew that I had to focus first and foremost on getting my education."

"When I was your age, I never did that!"

"I would never have talked to my mother the way that you talk to me."

"When I was in school, I always turned in my homework."

"When I was in school, I would never have kicked a hole in the wall!"

Although the statement, "Boys will be boys" is far too simplistic to explain male behavior, recognizing differences between male and female physical and emotional development must be considered in developing gender-appropriate parenting strategies.

Mistake #2

We try to rationalize our children's behavior without getting to know our children.

"You know how children are today."

"He is just going through a phase; he will grow out of it."

"He is hyperactive; he just cannot sit still."

"She has a learning disability."

"His attention span is so short, he just cannot concentrate."

"She is not very good at math. I was not very good at math either."

"He is just like his daddy!"

If you want to keep your ship from sinking do not make either of these mistakes. Get to know your child and share what you know with your child's teachers. The best way to help your

child is by establishing a relationship with your
child's teachers and developing a parent-teacher
partnership. When teachers tell us that our son
is misbehaving or not doing his schoolwork or
not following instructions, without offering
suggestions as to what we can do to help him,
they are just adding to our level of frustration.
Developing a parent-teacher partnership requires
that you share what you observe at home. In
turn, teachers must share what they observe
about your child at school. This goes far beyond
"what is wrong" to looking for what is right!

Observing your child

Your child's teachers observe your child's
behavior when he or she is away from you
and the influences of your household. He
or she may exhibit a different personality,
may engage in different types of interactions
with others, and may demonstrate interests
that are very different than what he or she
demonstrates at home. Equally important, he
or she may respond best to written versus
verbal instructions (learning style). He or she
may learn best through stories and anecdotes
versus lecturing (teaching style). He or she
may work best in groups with quiet and soft-
spoken children who take into account the

feelings of other group members (personality type). And, he or she may internalize what he or she has learned best when he or she can demonstrate, illustrate, write a rap, or give an oral presentation (Multiple Intelligences). On the other hand, his or her brother or sister may be slightly different or entirely different.

Despite whatever challenges you may have had in the past, you can better understand each of your children. While it does take some time, it can be done. Our two sons are exactly opposite in their personality types. They respond differently to verbal instructions. They have very different interests. Having grown up in the same household with the same parents, they have very different ways of doing and understanding things.

Our older son, Mychal-David, is highly visual. Our younger son, Jalani, is highly verbal. Each of them has their respective morning responsibilities. With my wife running a publishing company, and my speaking and travel schedule, our house is fast-paced in the mornings. The only way that we all cope is through regular routines and clear responsibilities.

Mychal-David and Jalani have each had a list of morning and evening responsibilities during the school week that we adjusted for each level of schooling (i.e., elementary, middle, and high school).

Following was Jalani's morning list throughout elementary school:

6:00 a.m.   *Say prayers and make-up bed*
6:10 a.m.   *Sit-ups and push-ups*
6:15 a.m.   *Wash up*
6:20 a.m.   *Eat breakfast*
6:35 a.m.   *Brush teeth*
6:45 a.m.   *Get dressed and brush hair*
7:00 a.m.   *Go to the bus stop*

Our older son had a similar list throughout elementary and middle school. Now, a high school senior, he has graduated from his list, however my wife and I make a mental note of the time that we wake him so he and his younger brother do not get into each other's way.

During the time when each of our sons had lists, they were posted onto the refrigerator so they could check off each completed task. At the end of the week their weekly allowance was tied directly to their success at fulfilling their daily responsibilities. While some might consider this too regimented, we know that it substantially reduced the stress level in our household. Furthermore, our younger son learned to read and tell time as part of the process of fulfilling his daily responsibilities.

Understanding our children's learning styles and intrinsic motivation, (i.e., auditory learner—playing with friends, visual learner—going to the skating rink), we gave them responsibilities and established a system of rewards and consequences that led them into developing the type of self-directed behavior needed to become successful in school.

Getting to know our children has helped us to become better parents. Parenting is a marathon, not a sprint. Steady, diligent, consistent effort will get you to the finish line. Take your time and learn a little day by day. It is during the day-to-day trials and tribulations of teaching and raising your children that you have so many wonderful opportunities to try new approaches. It may be as simple as giving written instructions, creating visuals of daily responsibilities, making better connections between rewards and consequences, providing your children with more opportunities for independent decision-making, changing your tone of voice, phrasing what you say differently, or at times not saying anything at all.

If your child is a visual learner and you give him all verbal instructions, no matter how much he wants to please you, and no matter how much you both want to be successful, he may not "understand" your instructions.

If your daughter has highly developed Verbal/Linguistic Intelligence, which is her primary means of processing what she learns, she may need to verbalize her thoughts and "tell" the story while reading. But if she is told, "Sit still and be quiet" or "Silently read to yourself" she may find reading difficult and frustrating.

If your son is a highly extraverted personality type and highly Verbal/Linguistic in his intelligence, he may find that working independently and in silence for long periods of time equally difficult and frustrating.

If your son is highly visual in his learning style and highly Bodily/Kinesthetic in his intelligence, he may find that doodling and frequent opportunities to move around provide the best opportunity for him to learn and to in fact enjoy the learning experience.

Get a journal

Get a journal or notebook and begin gathering information about each of your children. Just because you live in the same household and see your children every day does not mean that you know your children. Developing a better understanding of each of your children is a process, albeit painstaking, time-consuming, and frustrating.

Read the following questions. Using your journal, write down the answers to each of the questions as they pertain to your child:

1. Of the eight intelligences (identified by Dr. Howard Gardner), which are your child's dominant intelligences?

- *Verbal/Linguistic*
- *Logical/Mathematical*
- *Interpersonal*
- *Intrapersonal*
- *Visual/Spatial*
- *Musical/Rhythmic*
- *Bodily/Kinesthetic*
- *Naturalist*

2. Of the Myers-Briggs Personality Type Preferences, is your child more Introverted or Extraverted; Sensitive or Intuitive; Thinking or Feeling; Judging or Perceiving?

3. Is your child more Analytic or Global in his or her learning style?

4. Does your child appear to best understand by hearing, seeing, or doing?

5. What have been your child's best and worst learning situations in school?

6. What are your child's strengths, weaknesses, and intrinsic motivations?

7. How greatly is your child influenced by peer pressure?

8. What are your child's favorite hobbies, interests, subjects, and books?

9. What are your child's proudest accomplishments and achievements?

10. What are your child's dreams and aspirations?

Right now, you may be wondering what "Multiple Intelligences" have to do with little Patrice throwing a temper tantrum in the grocery store? Or, what "Analytic and Global learning styles" have to do with Myles being sent to "time-out" at school each day? Or, what CJ's "dreams and aspirations" have to do with the fact that he never does his homework, rarely completes his class work, and appears unconcerned by your taking away his television, computer, video games, and iPod?

Gathering and understanding the information needed to answer each of these questions will help you and your child's teachers to better understand how your child processes and applies knowledge; how to more effectively communicate with your child; how your child best learns; how to help your child make the connection between what he or she is learning in school to what he or she wants to achieve in life; and how to tap into the many areas of your child's intrinsic motivation. The more you learn about your child the more successful you will become at navigating the inevitable storms of parenting.

My wife and I have discovered that our older son is not only highly developed in his verbal, logical thinking, and illustrative abilities, but he is a highly visual learner. Whenever we gave him verbal instructions, he frequently forgot and was unsuccessful at following through. No matter how we disciplined him, took away privileges, or otherwise expressed our displeasure with his failure to be responsible, we were unsuccessful and he felt unsuccessful. In other words, "He just did not get it!"

When we began writing and listing all of his responsibilities step-by-step, together with consequences and expectations, he no longer had problems following instructions. When he could "see" the steps, when he could refer to the list to ensure that he had done all that he was expected to do, he was responsible and successful. We did not have to repeat ourselves. We simply said, "Look at the list." Whenever he asked to get together with his friends or to watch television we simply said, "Have you done everything on your list?"

We also helped his teachers to understand that verbal instructions were not nearly as effective as written instructions, and, they should not rely on him to tell us about important things. Instead, he needed a note to bring home; not every now and then, or when the situation had gotten out of control. We needed a note to be sent home every day. We accomplished this by having all of his teachers initial his student agenda each day after class. It was his responsibility to write down all assignments and test dates. His teachers simply initialed that he had fulfilled his responsibility of writing the information down.

On the other hand, our younger son is highly verbal. He learns best when we tell him what we want him to do and have him verbally reaffirm what we told him. "Jalani, go into your room, take your clothes off, put your clothes into the clothes hamper, and get into the bathtub. Jalani, what are you going to do?"

"I am going to go into my room, take my clothes off, put my clothes into the clothes hamper, and get into the bathtub. Then, I can have some ice cream. Right, Mom?"

Make notes in your journal as you observe your children each day in different situations. As you purposefully observe your children you will begin to better understand them as divinely-unique individuals. You may need different strategies for each child based upon what you learn about each child. Do not teach them the same way unless they learn in the same way. Stop saying, "What is wrong with you?" and work harder to understand the unique personality which embodies who they are individually.

Do not attempt to gather all of this information at one time but over the scope of a lifetime! Or at least, during your child's years in school—from preschool until he or she graduates from high school.

Throughout a child's childhood, you are likely to witness changes in learning styles, personality types, and his of her dreams and aspirations. As he or she learns and grows and goes through adolescence, you will need to continually update your information. You will not only use this information at home to help your child become successful at doing his or her homework, fulfilling his or her household responsibilities, and following your instructions, but you will give this information to his or her principal and teachers.

Many of the areas you will be observing (i.e., personality, intelligences, learning styles, etc.) represent entire books in themselves. However, I believe the brief introductions and tables that follow will allow you to quickly begin the process of identifying the unique learning styles and personality types of each of your children which will prove helpful to your family and to each child's teachers.

Personality Types

The most important factor in your daughter's succeeding in school will be her personal relationships—the relationship between you and her; the relationship between her and her siblings; and, the relationships between her and the teachers, staff, and students in her school.

My wife and I work hard at helping our sons to develop healthy relationships:

- *We help them develop a spiritual foundation and relationship with God. Our values, beliefs, and approaches to problem-solving are based on our faith in God's Word.*

- *We help them to maintain a positive relationship with us, as parents, by teaching them to demonstrate respect in their tone of voice, mannerisms, body language, and behaviors when speaking or communicating to us.*

- *We help them to develop a positive relationship with each other. We do not tolerate put downs, sarcasm, fighting, or any disrespectful behavior toward each other.*

- *We help them to develop positive relationships with other adults. We reinforce the respect we believe they should demonstrate toward adults.*

- *We teach them integrity and to take responsibility for their actions. Any inappropriate behavior toward a teacher at school or while visiting someone's home is followed by both a written and verbal apology.*

- *We help them to develop positive relationships with other children by providing frequent opportunities to attend camps and participate in team sports and group activities.*

- *We help them learn how to resolve conflicts with their peers by developing a personal sense of right and wrong, and an understanding of choices and consequences.*

Helping our sons to develop positive relationships requires conscious modeling on our part. How we believe, trust in, and speak about our relationship with God, how we speak to and deal with conflicts between each other, and how we speak about and deal with the many hurdles and obstacles in our lives all provide examples of the relationships, attitude, and behaviors that we want them to develop.

My wife and I have learned that the relationship between us, as husband and wife; the relationship between each of us and each of our sons; the relationship between our sons and each other; the relationship between us and our sons' teachers; and the relationship between our sons and their teachers can be better understood, and possibly strengthened, through understanding personality types.

As you go through each of the Personality Type tables, you may discover that you and your children frequently fall somewhere in the middle. Think in terms of the most common traits seen in each of you. Also, keep in mind that we often demonstrate personality traits at our jobs or at school which may be very different from those we demonstrate at home or with friends.

For example, when I speak to parents, teachers, and students, I demonstrate highly extraverted personality traits (i.e., I talk a lot, I approach people and initiate conversations, and I initiate relationships). However, my natural personality is highly introverted (i.e., I generally do not initiate conversations with strangers, I am uncomfortable at social events and in large gatherings, and I offer personal opinions only when asked).

My wife, on the other hand, is highly extraverted in social situations (i.e., life of the party, easily talks to and gets to know others, and initiates conversations). In professional situations, she is much more introverted (i.e., offers opinions only when brought into the discussion and is uncomfortable speaking in front of large groups).

As you review the Personality Type tables consider the following:

- Identify the personality traits you demon-strate at work or in work-related situations as opposed to the personality traits you demonstrate around family and friends.

- Identify the personality traits your children demonstrate at home as opposed to the personality traits they demonstrate in their classrooms, in their special interest or extracurricular activities, and with friends.

Understanding the uniqueness of each of your children's personalities will help you strengthen the relationship and build the bridge of communication with and between each child. No longer will you be able to say, "I do not understand you!" Your challenge will now be, "Now that I understand you, what am I going to do to help us communicate better?"

Your children's personality types will affect the relationships they develop with teachers and how well they function within their classrooms. Consider the following:

Your child is a highly-introverted personality type. She does not easily participate in classroom discussions unless she feels comfortable and supported by other students. She learns best when working independently in a quiet environment where discussions are held after an initial phase of quiet time.

However, in her classroom, the teacher is a highly-extraverted personality type who talks constantly. She believes that it is important for students to work in groups and talk a lot. Students frequently express their opinions by shouting. *Students ridicule opinions that differ from their own and frequently laugh at or put down other students. The teacher does not feel that this should hinder anyone from participating and, in fact, bases 30 percent of the grade on classroom participation. While your daughter does well on all of the written work, she fails miserably on group work and in classroom discussions. The highly-extraverted teacher feels there is something wrong with your highly-introverted daughter. By the end of the school year, your daughter's grades have dropped, her self-esteem has been lowered, and she feels inadequate and incapable. Her peers call her a "geek" and she, in fact, agrees with her teacher, "There is something wrong with me!"*

On the following Personality Type tables, adapted from the book, *Gifts Differing: Understanding Personality Type,* by Isabel Briggs Myers and Peter B. Myers, check or circle those personality traits which best describe you. Do the same for each of your children.

[Note: The term <u>Extravert</u> is commonly referred to as <u>Extrovert</u> in contemporary literature on temperament. I prefer to use the term <u>Extravert</u> as was originally used in the Myers-Briggs Type Indicator.]

A child's personality type preferences are likely to change as he or she undergoes the many physical-emotional changes from infancy through adulthood.

Parenting strategies must take into account the differences in the preschool, elementary, middle, and high school child.

Personality Types Table

Extravert (75% of population):

- Likes variety, action, and working with others.

- Easily meets, gets to know, talks to and socializes with others.

- Prefers interacting with people and talking while working.

- Easily communicates thoughts and ideas in lively, even loud discussions, where people frequently interrupt others.

- Frequently talks about things (often unrelated) as soon as it enters their mind no matter how often they interrupt others.

- Words that describe the Extravert: *Sociability • Interaction • External • Breadth • Extensive • Multiplicity of relationships • External events*

Introvert (25% of population):

- Likes quiet, uninterrupted time for focusing and concentrating.

- Does not easily meet new people. Has trouble remembering names and faces.

- Prefers interacting with ideas and talking after completing tasks.

- Difficulty articulating ideas and opinions in large group settings without clearly-defined rules for participation.

- Does not like to be interrupted when sharing thoughts, ideas, and opinions.

- Words that describe the Introvert: *Territorial • Concentration • Internal • Depth • Intense • Limited relationships • Conservation of energies*

Personality Types Table

Sensitive (75% of population):

- Prefers regular assignments and consistency.
- Prefers working through things step by step.
- Wants to know exactly what needs to be done before starting a project.
- Patient with routine details but impatient when details become complicated.
- Prefers an established way of doing things and is rarely driven by inspiration.
- Feels good about things already learned and avoids learning new tasks or ways of doing things.
- Words that describe the Sensitive: *Experience* • *Past* • *Realistic* • *Perspiration* • *Actual* • *Down-to-earth* • *Utility* • *Fact* • *Practicality* • *Sensible*

Intuitive (25% of population):

- Likes solving new problems.
- Prefers working on a variety of things.
- Does not like wasting time talking, is anxious to get started.
- Does not like working on repetitive tasks and frequently thinks about how to redesign, improve, or change a task.
- Constantly explores new ways of doing things and is driven by inspiration.
- Feels good about solving new problems and continually expanding knowledge.
- Words that describe the Intuitive: *Hunches* • *Future* • *Speculative* • *Inspiration* • *Possible* • *Head in clouds* • *Fantasy* • *Fiction* • *Ingenious* • *Imaginative*

Personality Types Table

Thinking (50% of population):

- Does not usually show feelings. Prefers dealing with facts rather than feelings.

- Would prefer to know what others think rather than how they feel.

- May unintentionally hurt other people feelings.

- Likes analysis, order, and does not mind figuring things out and being in charge.

- Does not mind sharing their thoughts and ideas without regard to how other people feel.

- Is more analytical, focusing on thoughts.

- Words that describe Thinkers: *Objective • Principles • Policy • Laws • Criterion • Firmness • Impersonal • Justice • Categories • Standards • Critique • Analysis*

Feeling (50% of population):

- Is aware of other people feelings and may overlook facts to avoid hurting someone's feelings.

- Would prefer to know how someone feels rather than what they think.

- Likes harmony. Wants things to work smoothly without conflict.

- Does not handle personal conflicts well and may be upset long after an argument.

- May be hurt by constructive criticism.

- Is more sympathetic, focusing on feelings.

- Words that describe Feelers: *Subjective • Values • Extenuating circumstances • Intimacy • Persuasion • Personal • Humane • Harmony • Good or Bad • Appreciate • Sympathy*

Personality Types Table

Judging (50% of population):

- Works best when they can plan their work and follow their plan.

- Likes to reach closure. Wants to complete projects, resolve issues, and move on.

- Does not take long to make up mind. Satisfied with their judgment or decision.

- Upon completion of one project, is eager to move onto another.

- Does not like interruptions and may lose sight of small details.

- Words that describe Judgers: *Settled* • *Decided* • *Fixed* • *Plan ahead* • *Closure* • *Decision-making* • *Planned* • *Completed* • *Decisive* • *Wrap it up* • *Urgency* • *Deadline!* • *Get the show on the road*

Perceiving (50% of population):

- May not plan well and does not mind working on projects without a clear plan or constantly changing conditions.

- Does not mind leaving things incomplete and open for changes.

- May have trouble making decisions. Open to reopening discussions or revisiting issues.

- May jump from project to project leaving all open and incomplete.

- Words that describe Perceivers: *Pending* • *Gather more data* • *Flexible* • *Let life happen* • *Open ended* • *Tentative* • *Something will turn up* • *There is plenty of time* • *Wait and see what happens*

After identifying the personality type preferences for yourself and each of your children, take time and discuss the commonalities and differences. Discuss the types of things you might do as a family to allow for and appreciate each other's differences. To better understand how to more effectively communicate with your children, read *Gifts Differing: Understanding Personality Type,* by Isabel Briggs Myers and Peter B. Myers, and *Please Understand Me: Character & Temperament Types,* by David Keirsey and Marilyn Bates.

The information on the following two pages, taken from the book, *Gifts Differing: Understanding Personality Type,* will help you and your child's teachers better understand how your child's personality types will affect how he or she learns, how eagerly he or she participates in classroom projects and discussions, and what types of things are needed to ensure that he or she feels successful within his or her respective classrooms.

Sensing and Intuitives
in the Classroom

"Type" makes a natural and predictable difference in learning styles and in students' responses to teaching methods. An understanding of "type" can help to explain why some students catch on to a way of teaching and like it, whereas others do not catch on and do not like it. Two distinct problems are involved here. Catching on is a matter of communication. Liking it is a matter of interest.

Communication from teacher to student begins with the spoken word in the classroom, where the student must be able to listen effectively, and later includes the written word in textbooks, which the student must be able to read. Because words, the necessary medium of education, have to be translated from symbols into meaning by the listener's intuition, the translation is naturally easier for intuitives than for sensing types. Intuitives use their favorite kind of perception, but sensing types have to use their less-liked, less-developed kind of perception, which takes more time and effort, especially when the words are abstract.

It is fortunate that the teacher [or parent] has control of how fast the words go by. Recognizing how much the sensing children need time to take in and understand words, the teacher can speak more slowly and pause after each sentence. Intuitive children will use the pause to add thoughts to what was said. Sensing children will use it to make sure they understand the teacher's words. Each sentence will then be effectively communicated to all the children.

Extraverts and Introverts in the Classroom

Essential to any reading method is the reassurance that letters stand for sounds and, therefore, a printed word shows the reader what it would sound like if it were spoken. The translation of sound-symbols is easiest for introverts with intuition. In first grade, the IN [Introversion plus Intuition] students are likely to be the quickest to catch on to the symbols and often are delighted with them. But the extravert children with sensing, the ES [Extravert plus Sensing] students, who make only minimal use of either intuition or introversion, may find the symbols so confusing that they become discouraged about the whole business of going to school. They may even decide, hopelessly or defiantly, that school is not for them.

Confusion about symbols is a very serious matter. Children of any type are doomed to flounder in school if they do not learn the meanings of the symbols by which language is written and must be read. They will be poor readers or nonreaders, depending on the depth of their confusion. They will do badly on achievement tests and intelligence tests. They will probably be bored by what they do not understand and may well be humiliated because they do not understand it. They tend to drop out of school as soon as possible. Their failures may be blamed on low IQs or perhaps on emotional difficulty, whereas actually, the failures and the low IQ and the emotional difficulty could all result from one omission. Nobody helped them, in the beginning, to learn the explicit meanings of the sound-symbols.

Multiple Intelligences

Dr. Howard Gardner, of Harvard University published a book, *Frames of Mind: The Theory of Multiple Intelligences,* in 1983, which outlined his theory of Multiple Intelligences. He outlined seven (since expanded to eight) areas in which each of us can acquire and demonstrate knowledge (be smart). Each individual has all eight areas of intelligence, however, no two individuals utilize the same combination of intelligences in the same way. For example, one child is better at understanding people while another is better at problem-solving, one child is better at singing or playing an instrument while another is better at sports or dance.

Make notes in your journal as you observe how your child appears to best learn and to apply what he or she knows. Think of a child's Multiple Intelligences as:

- *the many ways in which he or she <u>learns</u> how to do something;*

- *the many ways in which he or she <u>actually does</u> what he or she has learned; and*

- *the many ways in which he or she demonstrates talents, gifts, or abilities.*

When you review the Multiple Intelligences tables, ask yourself the following questions:

1. Does my child appear to best *remember* what was taught:

    - *when talking or writing about what was learned? (Word smart: Verbal/Linguistic)*

    - *when developing a series of steps or solving problems? (Problem-solving smart: Logical/ Mathematical)*

    - *when moving around or constructing a model? (Body smart: Bodily/Kinesthetic)*

    - *when performing a rap, singing a song, or tapping out a beat in his or her head? (Music smart: Musical/Rhythmic)*

    - *when working in groups and engaging in discussions? (People smart: Interpersonal)*

    - *when working alone with time for self-reflection, internalizing, and focusing? (Self smart: Intrapersonal)*

    - *when doodling, designing, illustrating, or drawing pictures? (Picture smart: Visual/ Spatial)*

    - *when sitting, walking, discussing, or studying outdoors? (Environmentally smart: Naturalist)*

2. Does my child appear to best *demonstrate* what he or she has learned when he or she can:

    - *draw a picture?*
    - *write a paper or tell a story?*
    - *solve the problem?*
    - *sing a song?*
    - *build, design, or invent something?*
    - *share feelings with others?*
    - *engage in self-reflection?*
    - *present an outdoor demonstration?*

3. Does my child appear to have a "natural gift" of, or be self-motivated to learn more about:

    - *talking or writing?*
    - *problem-solving?*
    - *drawing or designing?*
    - *working with other people?*
    - *intuition and self-reflection?*
    - *music?*
    - *sports, dance, or inventing?*
    - *activities relating to nature (e.g., fishing, camping, hiking, rock climbing, examining animals and insects, observing cloud formations, or bird watching)?*

The Multiple Intelligence information that you gather will help you to better understand how your children are smart. Children who are good in music, art, or sports have always been called "gifted" or "talented," but not necessarily "smart." Athletes have always been called "jocks" (sometimes jokingly referred to as "dumb jocks"). Their athletic abilities were identified simply as representing athletic prowess, gifts, or natural abilities. Now we know that their abilities, as demonstrated in their respective sports, represent the highest form of Bodily/Kinesthetic Intelligence.

While the Bodily/Kinesthetic Intelligence of the athlete might be his or her most dominant intelligence, it is not the only intelligence he or she can develop.

David Robinson, former professional basketball player, Olympic Goal Medalist, and NBA Most Valuable Player for the San Antonio Spurs, plays classical piano, scored highly on the SAT, graduated with honors from the United States Naval Academy, and is recognized as a computer genius. His intelligences have been developed far beyond the Bodily/Kinesthetic Intelligence demonstrated through his skills on the basketball court.

Your son, the aspiring football player, can develop the Logical/Mathematical Intelligence needed to invest his money; the Interpersonal

Intelligence needed to be an effective team player; the Verbal/Linguistic Intelligence required to go into broadcast journalism; and/or the Intrapersonal Intelligence needed to remain spiritually centered and at peace within himself.

These are the many ways in which children are smart; ways in which children acquire, process, and apply knowledge.

Consider the following:

Your child is a highly visual learner and has highly developed Visual/Spatial Intelligence. You know this because your child doodles while the teacher is talking, remembers best when the teacher uses charts, graphs, or pictures, and appears to be most successful at following written instructions. Your child easily illustrates pictures and appears to best remember those stories that he or she illustrates after reading the story. Your child "sees" something and easily remembers all of the details. Your child spends his or her free time drawing or painting. Your child is drawn to books that have pictures, e.g., illustrated stories, comic books, video game books, fashion magazines, etc.

Your child's teacher, however, is highly verbal. She rarely writes things on the board. She "tells" children what she wants them to do and holds them responsible for accurately writing down what she says. She does not like children doodling while she is talking. She accepts written assignments only and does not encourage children to draw or illustrate concepts, create collages, or provide other opportunities to demonstrate what they have learned. Her classroom is full of words; no posters, pictures, or visual images.

When your child fails in her classroom, the teacher tells you that your child has a problem and suggests that your child's low grades and test scores indicate that your child may have a learning disability.

The problem here is not necessarily that the teacher is not an effective teacher for some children. The problem is that she is not an effective teacher for your child unless she is willing to consciously expand her teacher style to better accommodate your child's learning style. All of this could have been avoided if you had been able to share the information about your child and the possible mismatch of teaching style to your child's learning style with the teacher and principal. You could have avoided your child's low academic achievement, lowered self-esteem, and lack of learning by letting the principal and the teacher know, "My child is a highly visual learner with a highly-developed Visual/Spatial Intelligence."

Parents and teachers frequently spend too much time focused on a child's deficits rather than on their assets. They look at a child's weaknesses and predict failure rather than focusing on a child's strengths and predicting success. Despite having a highly-developed Logical/Mathematical Intelligence I failed chemistry three times; once in high school and twice in college. If I would have defined myself by my failure in chemistry I may have missed my gifts in writing. While failing chemistry may have been a good indicator that I would not become a chemistry teacher or a chemist, it had nothing to do with my ability to succeed in life.

Most people are highly developed in only two or three of the eight intelligences. Some children are better at problem-solving while others are better at working with people. Some children are better at writing and speaking while others are better at sports or building things. Help your children to appreciate their strengths, their gifts, and their uniqueness. Use programs, camps, and activities to continually nurture and develop each child's unique gifts, talents, abilities, and areas of interest. While validating and appreciating their strengths, help them to understand and develop their weaknesses. Biceps and triceps, abdominal and back represent complimentary muscle groups. While either may be stronger than the other, we must consciously develop both for symmetry and stability. So too, must each child continue to develop his or her gifts while consciously strengthening his or her weaknesses.

Review the Multiple Intelligences tables on the following pages. Check or circle those areas which appear to be the most dominant areas in each of your children and then do the same for yourself.

Identify summer camps and after-school programs to provide further opportunities for your child to explore and develop his or her gifts.

Our children have attended martial arts camps, in-line skating camps, football camps, Space Camp, participated in little league baseball, AAU Track and Field competitions, and a wide range of YMCA youth programs. Our older son spent one summer in Bermuda studying marine biology and another at Dartmouth College in a business and leadership development program. Our children have also been in after-school programs in art, acting, and computer animation.

Each experience provides an opportunity to develop a gift and to inspire a dream.

Multiple Intelligences Table

Verbal/Linguistic

Good at memorizing names, places, and dates, and at writing or speaking.

Learns best by saying, hearing, and seeing words.

Logical/Mathematical

Good at math, reasoning, logic, problem-solving, and strategy games.

Learns best by categorizing, classifying, working with abstract patterns/relationships.

Interpersonal

Understands people, good at working with others, organizing, and mediating conflicts.

Learns best by sharing, comparing, relating, cooperating, and interviewing.

Intrapersonal

Spiritually centered. Understands self and own feelings. Focuses on self and personal development.

Learns best by working alone, through individualized projects, self-paced instruction, having own space.

Multiple Intelligences Table (cont.)

Bodily/Kinesthetic

Works well with hands. Good at sports, dancing, acting, video games, or building things.

Learns best by touching, moving, processing knowledge through bodily sensations or by doing.

Musical/Rhythmic

Ear for tones, picking up sounds, or remembering melodies. Sings, hums, or plays an instrument.

Learns best through rhythm, melodies, and music.

Visual/Spatial

Good at drawing, designing, or creating things. Also, imagining things, reading maps, mazes, puzzles, and charts.

Learns best by visualizing, working with colors and pictures.

Naturalist

Deep understanding of the outdoors, cloud patterns, rock formations, or animals.

Learns best by being outdoors or in the natural environment using all of the senses.

We have helped our older son, who is highly Visual and highly Verbal, strengthen these areas. During the summer between fifth and sixth grades we encouraged him to set aside time for drawing, reading, and writing each day. We also talked to him each day about his weak Interpersonal Intelligence (as demonstrated by his language and behaviors toward his younger brother) and helped him to consciously make better choices as he developed better people skills.

Our younger son, as is the case with many young children, was eager to develop all of his intelligences. He stretched his Verbal/Linguistic Intelligence through his intrinsic desire to talk "all of the time." We used his interest in talking to lead him into reading, storytelling, and dramatizing the stories which he read. His passion for sports and video game playing led him into developing his Bodily/Kinesthetic Intelligence. His natural desire to sing, dance, problem-solve, and play with others made it easy for us to help him expand his intelligence in many different and diverse areas.

Learning Styles

While Multiple Intelligences represent entire intellectual domains through which we apply intelligence and understand life, Learning Styles reflect how we "best learn." The Global and Analytic Learning Styles tables have been adapted from the book, *Bringing Out The Giftedness in Your Child,* by Rita Dunn, Kenneth Dunn, and Donald Treffinger. They outline both learning styles and learning situations. Another helpful book is, *Awakening Your Child's Natural Genius*, by Thomas Armstrong. After reviewing the tables, ask yourself the following questions:

- does my child appear to learn best by "seeing";

- by "hearing"; or

- by "doing" (touching or building)?

Completing these tables will provide greater insight into the divinely-unique person, who is your child. Use this information to strengthen your relationship with each of your children. Help them to appreciate the uniqueness of how they learn, how they apply what they know, and who they are. As a guide, in the Appendix are tables containing the information my wife and I have gathered for each of our sons. We have continually referred to and updated this information each school year.

Learning Styles Table

Global

The greatest challenge in teaching global learners is
not to bore them. They appear to learn best through
stories, humor, and pictures. Following are some of
the situations in which global learners appear most
comfortable:

- Prefer hearing a story or watching a movie or
  play.
- Prefer noise while working (music, tv, or
  talking).
- Prefer to work in groups where they talk while
  they work.
- Appear to learn best from the interaction
  with other children (particularly with similar
  interests and talents) rather than from direct
  adult supervision and instruction.
- Prefer to talk while eating.
- Prefer informal seating for learning (e.g., bean
  bag, pillow, rocking chair, bed, carpet, etc.).
- Prefer working on several things at a time with
  breaks in between.
- Remember most of what is said without taking
  notes. Learns best when "told" what to do.

Learning Styles Table (cont.)

Analytic

Analytic learners appear to learn most easily when information is introduced step-by-step or fact-by-fact. Following are some of the situations in which analytic learners appear most comfortable:

- Prefer things to be quiet.
- Prefer to work in groups where they talk after they work.
- Prefer to talk after eating.
- Prefer bright lights and formal seating like desk, table, or chair.
- Prefer working on one thing at a time and completing tasks.
- Prefer taking notes while the teacher is talking.
- Learns best when instructions are written.

Additional Learning Styles

- Auditory: Learns best by hearing.
- Kinesthetic: Learns best by doing.
- Tactile: Learns best by touching.
- Visual: Learns best by seeing.

Additional information you should gather and share with your children's teachers are their:

- best and worst learning situations in school;

- strengths, weaknesses, and intrinsic motivation;

- favorite hobbies, interests, subjects, and books;

- proudest accomplishments and achievements; and

- dreams, aspirations, and personal goals.

Provide the information to each of your children's teachers and update your lists with whatever you learn about your children during the course of each school year. Since preschool, we have witnessed the personality type of our older son undergo dramatic changes. We do not know if the extraverted, highly-verbal young man who was our son in preschool, despite our best efforts as parents, was chased away by teachers who saw only problems instead of his gifts; teachers who smothered his personality as a result of how his personality conflicted with their own, and who could not keep up with him, and therefore slowed him down, or, if his personality just naturally changed as a result of growing older and discovering more about himself and being influenced by his friends. (We suspect a little of both.) We noticed, as a seventh-grader, his personality move from introversion to extraversion. Outspoken, articulate, and very popular amongst his peers, we witnessed yet another transformation.

During most school years we have experienced that by providing our sons' teachers with the information we have gathered, they have appreciated the information and have demonstrated a willingness to work with us to help our sons to be engaged academically and nurtured socially within their classrooms. We have also experienced that even when my wife and I provide all of our information to our sons' schools, there may not be a teacher at their respective grade level who teaches or who has a classroom that is structured in a way that is suited to how our sons best learn. However, by knowing what our sons' needs are, we are better able to help their teachers (some more than others) help each of them to be successful in school. In the case of our older son, we found that while math was a strength throughout elementary and middle school, he needed tutors for both his honors Algebra II and honors Pre-Calculus classes in high school.

While it is possible that a parent's learning style will be similar to that of their children, it is also possible that the two learning styles will be entirely different between parent and child and between any two children in the same family. Children learn by concentrating on, absorbing, using, and ultimately *processing* information. Your child's learning style is the primary method by which he or she absorbs information. His or her intelligences represent the primary means by which he or she processes and uses that information. While you can force your child to learn and to apply what he or she knows in the ways in which you do, you can only help your child to achieve his or her divinely-given potential by helping him or her to further develop the natural processing styles that are uniquely his or her own.

I frequently speak to students about my experiences in school (*Follow Your Dreams: Lessons That I Learned in School*). After sharing the story of how I developed a passion for writing in the second grade I ask, "What is the best job that you could have?" After they have told me all of the popular, highly-paying, or prestigious jobs (e.g., doctor, lawyer, professional athlete, entertainer, etc.), I tell them, "The best job that you could have is to do what you love to do while getting paid to do it!"

As you better understand your child, help your child to better understand and value his or herself. Look for every opportunity to help he or she discover those dreams and aspirations that utilize his or her unique intellectual strengths, capitalize on his or her unique personality, and connect to his or her unique passions and areas of interest. Expose your child to the wide range of careers which may one day provide an opportunity for him or her to, "Do what he or she loves to do and get paid for doing it."

Teacher Strategies

Create "Parent Tips" for cultivating student success in your classroom, e.g., "How to encourage personal goal-setting (e.g., honor roll, extra credit, 'A's.')"; "How to ensure early intervention of homework completion and test preparation"; etc.

- Provide a checklist for effective organization, examples of effective note-taking, and sample tests/ quizzes.

- Provide sample Learning Styles, Multiple Intelligences, and Personality Type tables.

- Take student differences into account, e.g., gender, socioeconomic, preexisting knowledge, support mechanisms, etc., when creating assignments and developing grading rubrics and methodology.

S tep 2

Identify the Best School

D o not spend all of your time looking for schools with the highest test scores or high schools with the highest graduation rates and largest percentage of students who go on to college without spending time understanding your child. Being the highest-ranked school does not guarantee that a school will be the best school for your child or guarantee that your child will get the best teachers for her unique needs, ambitions, dreams, or aspirations.

Consider the first step of getting to know your child as the first piece of your parenting puzzle. All of the other pieces must now be put into place in relation to the first piece.

Would a child who is highly Verbal/ Linguistic be best served by a school that has no drama, speech and debate, writer's club, student newspaper or other outlet for her unique interests and abilities?

Would the child who is highly Bodily/ Kinesthetic be best served by a school that has no athletic, acting, dance, gymnastics, Drill Team, Marching Band, or other program which offers such a child the opportunity to showcase or further develop his Bodily/Kinesthetic Intelligence?

In the case of our older son, my wife and I researched the schools that would enhance his Visual/Spatial Intelligence and provide him with an environment where he could grow beyond the academic areas into the arts. While our son was attending the tenth highest academically-ranked elementary school in the state of Georgia, and would have been scheduled to attend the top academically-ranked middle and high school, the curriculum did not include extensive studies in the arts, particularly in his most gifted area, the visual arts. Although test data and graduation rates (his zoned high school had a 98 percent graduation rate) are important variables in looking at a school, they are not the only variables. Use the information that you have gathered about your child to help determine the best school for your child.

My wife and I have a commitment to public education. We believe that public schools can only become great schools when the public, whom they serve, commits to helping them become great schools. However, not even great public schools are great for all children. While our son's public school in Georgia, was a great school, with a great office staff, and great teachers, it was not the best possible school for our son.

Because of our commitment, first to our children and secondly to public education, we relocated from a 5,500 square foot, six-bedroom, four-bathroom home in the exclusive north Atlanta suburb of East Cobb County, Georgia, to a 672 square foot, two-bedroom, one-bathroom home in an impoverished area of St. Petersburg, Florida. At the time, our son was attending a top-ten ranked elementary school and was zoned to go into a top-ranked middle and high school.

However, our son's true gifts lay in the visual arts. Since first grade, his little stick people had taken shape and dimension and by fourth grade, with minimum professional instruction, he was becoming a gifted illustrator. My wife and I were doing all that we could to provide art classes after school and to enroll him in art camps during the summer, but he was not getting enough instruction during the school day. He had art one day per week for 35 minutes. In the middle school that he would have attended he would rotate through art classes for one grading period during the school year with no guarantee that he would be able to consistently enroll in the one art rotation during each grade.

We developed a plan in which we relocated to St. Petersburg, Florida, so that he could begin fifth grade in a public magnet school of the arts (Perkins Elementary). He would have a full hour of art each week, together with a full hour of graphic arts, and a full hour each week on the graphic layout and design of the school's literary magazine. While the school had a lottery system that allowed children to enroll from throughout the county, the only way our son could enroll would be if we lived in the zone surrounding the school. The zone was a largely impoverished area comprised of small homes, apartments, and public housing projects. The only house available for sale at the time was our little two-bedroom house.

Most of our family and friends considered our relocation drastic (some said, "foolish, stupid, ridiculous, and insane"). My wife and I accepted it as simply a part of our plan. While we lived in a picturesque community in Georgia, we had a child who was blessed with visually artistic talent (Visual/Spatial Intelligence). Although he was, admittedly, attending a great school in a great school system, his artistic talents and abilities would not have been nurtured or developed to the level of his potential.

We do not believe that other families should have to make such a drastic choice. Schools should be more nurturing of the various gifts, talents, and intelligences of children. However, until they are, each family must develop a plan based upon the unique talents, abilities, and needs of their children, and opportunities available within their local schools.

Our son will complete high school at North Springs High School in Atlanta, Georgia where he will receive both, the Visual and Performing Arts and Math and Science Magnet Seals of Distinction. He was accepted into Amherst College, in large part due to the strength of his art portfolio and the passionate pursuit of his dream since elementary school.

Help the school help your child

After determining the school that would best work *for* your child you must work with teachers within the school to help them to best work *with* your child. While principals and teachers generally *want* the best for your child, only by collaborating with them can you entrust them to *know* what is best for your child and *do* what is in the best interest of your child.

My wife and I have met and worked with some of the best principals and teachers in schools throughout the country. For the most part, our own children have gone to schools that have had good principals and they have been taught by good teachers. However, by being actively involved and by sharing the information gathered in the previous step with our sons' principals and teachers, we have increased the odds of our sons experiencing success in school.

I do not believe that you should distrust your child's school. People in public education certainly are not in it for the money. I believe that most teachers want to do the best for children and that most teachers sincerely want to do all they can to help children learn. However, I cannot say that all teachers are good teachers because I know some who are not. I cannot say that all teachers care about children because I know some who do not.

As a parent, and as my child's advocate, I will not entrust my child's future to a stranger! While there are a lot of good teachers, I approach my children's teachers each year with what I consider healthy skepticism.

Each school year my child's teachers are the doctors responsible for operating on my child's brain for the next nine months. I am going to present them with all of the information I have gathered about each of my children and I want to become a partner in the medical treatment (teaching) of my children. Since my child's teachers are the doctors, I want to be the assisting surgeon. I care more about each of my children's teacher's willingness to become a partner with me in their learning than in how long he or she has been teaching.

My wife and I both believe that how much our children learn and how successful they are in school is based in large part on the relationship <u>they</u> have with their teachers, and on the relationship <u>we</u> have with their teachers.

Whenever you have a choice of schools, camps, programs, or activities you must raise the question, "How are children like my child performing in this school, program, or activity?"

You have a responsibility to your child to get to know everything you can about the school and the people in it. Do not allow anyone to make you feel unwelcome in your child's school or to suggest that they are doing you a favor by allowing your child to attend school there. Always remember that good schools welcome parental involvement. Good teachers welcome the opportunity to become partners with parents in their child's education. Good teachers invite people to look at how and what they teach because good teachers provide good classroom instruction and you can see learning taking place.

Gather information about the school

Despite the fact that many schools may not be open and straight forward in providing the information you need to help ensure that your child has a successful school year, getting to know your child's school is a lot easier than you may think.

Get a box, a file cabinet, a drawer, or identify a place in your home you can devote solely to keeping information related to your child's school. Get into the habit of placing *all* school related information into this box. As soon as it comes home, whether or not you have an opportunity to review it at the time, place it into the box. At the end of each school year, seal these boxes, mark the grade, and store them away (one day when your children become adults they will thank you).

Get a notebook, note pad, journal, or folder to use exclusively for your child's school. Use it to make notes, write down names, and keep track of any information that will help you to get to know your child's school and its people.

Gather as much information about the school as you can:

- student achievement, class enrollment, and extracurricular activity participation data;

- addresses, phone numbers, fax numbers, e-mail addresses, and web page addresses;

- names, e.g., superintendent, school board representative, principal, office staff, teachers, counselors, etc; and

- important dates, e.g., yearly calendar, school holidays, testing dates, report card dates, and registration dates.

Which teachers' teaching style best matches your youngsters' learning style strengths? Why should you pressure your child's school principal for the best possible student–teacher instructional match? Because one year of "lost" schooling is rarely regained, and "turning off" a child is exactly what must <u>not</u> happen!

[Bringing Out the Giftedness in Your Child]

Find out what has been written in local newspapers about your child's school. Many local newspapers post the state or local ranking of schools based on test scores. They also post data for dropout rates and college admission rates for high schools. Check the local library and ask the librarian for help. Make copies of newspaper articles and ask the school for copies of such things as published test data, discipline data, and graduation rates for high schools. Get a copy of the school's *"School Improvement Plan"* or, *"State Report Card."* Most public schools are required to publish an *AYP* (Annual Yearly Progress) report each school year which outlines the school's goals, objectives, and student achievement levels. There are web sites that post information about local schools, oftentimes with parents' and students' comments.

Attitudes toward children

Since our children are African-American boys, we want to know what percentage of the African-American children, and what percentage of boys, make the honor roll, qualify for the Talented and Gifted program, take AP (Advanced Placement) or honors classes, are involved in special programs and activities, are referred to the office, or have been suspended from school. This is often a sensitive issue for schools, particularly those whose data indicates that minority children, or boys, are disproportionately referred to the office or suspended from school. Rather than being sensitive people should be asking, "Why?" If a school, for whatever reasons, has identifiable groups of children (i.e., race, gender, ethnicity, socioeconomic background, etc.) who are underachieving or underrepresented in advanced classes, on the honor roll, in Talented and Gifted or academic enrichment programs, or in other types of special interest groups or activities, parents, teachers, coaches, counselors, and the school's principal should want to know why. If certain groups of students are being disproportionately referred to the office, suspended from school, placed into special education, prescribed medication, or experiencing behavioral problems, as a parent if my child falls into one of these groups I would want to know why? And, I would think that the school would want to know why as well.

Review the personality types, Multiple Intelligences, learning styles, and best learning situations you identified for your child. Any mismatches between a teacher's personality type or teaching style and your child's personality type and learning style could present a problem. As too, a teacher who has a negative perception or lower expectations of children due to their race, gender, or socioeconomic background. Remember that teachers are people. Perhaps you have heard people make such declarations as:

"You know, boys will be boys."

"We should have 'realistic' expectations for poor children."

"Boys are better at math and science."

"Black kids do not study or work as hard as white kids."

"Asian kids are always the smartest students in the school."

"Some kids should not think about college. They should concentrate on vocational or technical programs."

As a parent you may be guilty of making the same or similar declarations. It is human nature to stereotype others and to misunderstand those who look different, think differently, or who come from a different culture. There is a proverb that says, "What you say does not speak nearly as loudly as what you do!" While teachers may say, "I believe all children can learn," I am more interested in whether or not those children who look like, behave like, or learn like my child are, in fact, learning within their classrooms.

I find that most schools attempt the school year without having well-defined goals for what they expect for each student.

To me, it is so easy to declare what students cannot do, but I always tell the teachers who work here [Marva Collins' Westside Preparatory School] that a good teacher will always make the "poor" student good and the "good" student superior. The word teacher is a Latin word meaning "to lead or to draw out." The good teacher is always willing to polish and shine until the true shining luster of each student shines through.

["Ordinary" Children, Extraordinary Teachers]

At my son's elementary school, in St. Petersburg, Florida, despite a 30 percent minority student population, there was only one African-American child (my son) in the fifth grade Talented and Gifted Program. There were only two African-American children in my son's classroom (my son and one girl) who regularly qualified for the honor roll. Of the 14 children who regularly qualified for the honor roll, 85 percent were the same race as my son's teacher, 64 percent were the same gender, and 57 percent were the same race and gender. In classrooms, as in most households, males, typically identify with and relate better to males, and females, typically, identify with and relate better to females. The same holds true for members of one race and with the same sex within racial groups. Only by looking at such obvious disparities can we create more opportunities to ensure that ALL children are learning.

In the classrooms of some teachers, the <u>only</u> children who regularly qualify for the honor roll and achieve the highest grades are those children who look like the teacher! I heard one teacher remark in a workshop, "On the first day of school, I can usually tell which students will be my 'A students,' which ones will be my 'B students,' and which ones will be my 'C students.' In the twenty years that I have been teaching, I have only been wrong once." Do you think that the students who looked like "A students," also looked like her?

My wife and I want our children in the classrooms of teachers who have an "I can teach" attitude. Teachers who believe they can be successful teaching all children, who recognize any disparities in student achievement, and who, themselves, raise the question, "How can we ensure that all students are successful?"

School Climate & Culture

Every school and every classroom (every household as well) has a culture. As parents must foster a household culture of high expectations, so too, must teachers. Household culture, school culture, and classroom culture will all impact the achievement levels of your child. Of those three influences, classroom culture will have the greatest impact on your child's experiences in school. Teachers must understand and incorporate the real lives of their students (i.e., age, ability level, gender, ethnicity, culture, socioeconomic background, home environment, etc.) into the strategies utilized to foster a positive classroom climate and culture. The strategies a teacher utilizes in suburban Cobb County, Georgia, will be different from those utilized by a teacher in urban Chicago. As too, the strategies utilized by a middle school teacher are likely to be different from those utilized by a first-grade teacher.

The success of the classroom experience is analogous to that of any athletic team. Parents and the school have minimal influence on the success of the school's basketball team. The buck stops with the coaching staff. They determine the values; they foster the beliefs; they determine the most appropriate practice methods; they develop the strategies; and they are responsible for cultivating the "collaborative" effort" needed to win.

I coached youth (six- to eight-year-old) basketball in Carson, California, and, I coached youth (eight- to eleven-year-old) baseball in St. Petersburg, Florida. As was the case in Carson (where we went to the Parks and Recreation Championship each year), I had no control over who the players were or where they came from. The reality of the eleven players on my St. Petersburg baseball team was that three were under the care of grandparents; five were from single-parent households; one was involved in a court custody case that resulted in the beating death of his mother; four were from families living below the poverty level; and six were regularly in trouble at school.

Given the real lives of our players we had to develop strategies that were effective and appropriate for cultivating the environment we needed in order to help them to become successful. Nina (team mom), myself, and the other coach (another mom), developed strategies to foster a positive climate and culture. We got whistles so that no one had to scream at the children; we established clear rules (i.e., no put downs, no pushing or shoving, be on time, no unexcused absences, listen to the coaches, and maintain a positive attitude) and gave a copy of our team rules to each player; we established clear consequences for each rule infraction that was equitably enforced among all players; and we gave instructions to each player based on what we understood about their learning styles (we had children who had been labeled LD, EBD, and ADD).

Our team was the only team in the league with players who never laughed at, put down or otherwise verbally abused another team's players. Our team was polite, respectful, and consistently demonstrated good sportsmanship on the way to a 14-1 record. How our players performed and what they learned was a result of our willingness to develop strategies based on the reality of who they were individually without regard to making gender or race-based stereotypes, or pitying them.

The reality of individual classrooms and entire school communities is that the climate and culture is either defined, taught, and continually reinforced by the adults within the school community or it defaults to the children. As a parent I do not want my son defining the climate and culture of his classroom. I want the teacher to define, teach, model, and continually reinforce those values and behaviors which are consistent with cultivating an environment that is socially nurturing and has high academic expectations.

When you meet your child's teacher and discuss your concerns about the classroom. Be an advocate for your child, pointing out specific abilities, talents, or strengths and suggest ways in which these might be incorporated into the classroom day. Offer to serve as a volunteer in the class. Bring in innovative learning materials to enrich the classroom. Above all, work cooperatively and diplomatically. Teachers are under a lot of pressure these days and may feel like your sincere attempts to help your child are just another problem they have to confront. If the teacher sees your offers of assistance as an opportunity to lighten her own load, then you will probably succeed in changing the status quo for your child.

[In Their Own Way]

It does not matter how good a teacher is at instruction or how much a teacher knows about the subject matter; if he or she is not good at fostering a positive classroom climate and culture, free of bullying and put downs, which maximizes student time-on-task, students cannot reach their highest level of learning. Over the course of his years in school (pre-k through the twelfth grade), my wife and I have witnessed a direct correlation between our older son's enthusiasm about school, social experiences within the classroom, academic achievement, and his teacher's classroom management.

You must find an opportunity to go to your child's school. Whether you volunteer, attend PTA/PTSA meetings, attend student performances, have lunch with your child, or simply walk through the corridors and admire student work and awards. Whenever parents are involved in their child's school, their presence alone helps to cultivate a more orderly school community. Only through your involvement can you help to ensure that your children's schools develop a climate and culture which nurtures them socially and inspires them academically.

Following is a five-step plan for parents and teachers to positively influence the climate and culture in your household, in your child's school, and within your child's classroom.

After reviewing the following lists, observe your child's school and classroom to see what, if anything, is missing. Do what my wife and I have done—do not sit home and complain, get involved and help your child's school and teachers to develop a positive and nurturing environment for children. Your child, together with hundreds of other children, will spend 180 or more days in the school and within their respective classrooms.

Home

1. Develop your vision (i.e., what type of adult do you want your child to become?). Make a list of words which you envision being used to describe your son or daughter as an adult, e.g., spiritual, responsible, polite, kind, compassionate, trustworthy, honest, diligent, determined, resilient, persistent, persevering, confident, self-motivated, respectable, intelligent, etc.

2. Consciously define, articulate, and continually reinforce the values and beliefs consistent with achieving your vision. These values and beliefs may include:

    *   no put downs, sarcasm, or negative language;

    *   using polite language (e.g., excuse me, thank you, please) and demonstrating positive behaviors;

    *   respect for self and others;

    *   personal responsibility and persistence;

    *   not making excuses; and

    *   responsibly performing homework and chores before play time.

Additionally:

- identify, post, and continually reinforce short- and long-term goals;

- post your child's academic and achievement awards throughout your home; and

- recognize, praise, reward, and value academic achievement as you would athletic or performance-related accomplishments.

3. Enroll your child in youth programs (e.g., martial arts, YMCA youth programs, summer camps, church programs, etc.) and encourage your child to read books and materials that reinforce the values promoted through those programs and which reinforce your values and beliefs.

4. Provide uninterrupted time for homework and studying (i.e., no phone calls, visitors, television, or video games) together with easy access to books, materials, and supplies to complete homework and prepare for tests.

5. Regularly recognize and celebrate your child's success in demonstrating the values and beliefs that you are attempting to foster (i.e., diligence, determination, personal responsibility, perseverance, kindness, compassion, etc.).

A Parent's Vision

My vision for our household is that everyone will enjoy the freedom to openly and honestly express their feelings, emotions, ideas, and opinions as long as it is done in a respectful and concerned manner and does not hurt or offend others. As a family we will work to provide a safe, loving, caring, and supportive environment. We will encourage each other in developing and pursuing our individual and collective dreams. Each member of our family will have a role to play and a responsibility to fulfill in supporting the individual and collective vision of our family.

As your parent(s) I/we must do our best to provide a positive model, through our example, of those personal qualities and characteristics that are consistent with achieving our vision; such character traits as diligence, determination, commitment, responsibility, and dependability. We must also demonstrate guidance, leadership, and support through praising those behaviors and actions that are expected and through disciplining those behaviors and actions which are unacceptable and considered detrimental to achieving the highest possible level of individual and/or collective success and prosperity.

As children, we expect you to recognize your role within our family and your responsibility to the world around you. Personal qualities such as honor, compassion, courage, and integrity cannot be given nor taken away, but will help you to become a person to be admired and respected by others. In more ways than we can count, the world is crying out for people who will make a difference in societal issues, the environment, humanitarianism, justice, peace, and moral leadership. Our vision is that each of us will in some way make a difference.

School

1. Verbally affirm and visually display the school's mission, vision, and beliefs.

2. Follow the "4Cs" (caring, clarity, commitment, and consistency) to articulate and reinforce the values and beliefs of the school's vision and guiding principles throughout the school community.

3. Reinforce the school's values and beliefs through instructional activities (language arts, performances, reading, writing, classroom discussions, assemblies, etc.) and through visual images (cups, flags, buttons, T-shirts, bumper stickers, etc.).

4. Foster teacher collaboration to ensure instructional practices and classroom management strategies are consistent with achieving the school's vision.

5. Verbally and visually reinforce the school's values and beliefs throughout the school community:

   • Post words, phrases, language, and visual images.

- Portray the school's mascot in situations displaying the school's values and beliefs.

- Make daily announcements to recognize student behavior; achieving attendance and tardy goals; academic achievement; and student success.

- Utilize bulletin boards, trophy cases, assemblies, recognition programs, banners, T-shirts, school letters, sweaters, the school newspaper, etc., to recognize students who embody the school's values and beliefs.

- Host regular school-wide celebrations to recognize and celebrate the varied areas of student achievement (i.e., citizenship, arts, scholarly, and athletic).

- Host staff, parent, volunteer, and business partner recognition programs.

- Create effective intervention and prevention programs to teach students that verbal, physical, or sexual harassment within the school community is in direct conflict with the school's values and beliefs.

What I Won't Do for My Friends

1. I won't steal for my friends.

2. I won't cheat for my friends.

3. I won't act dumb for my friends.

4. I won't do drugs for my friends.

5. I won't disrupt the class for my friends.

6. I won't disrespect, laugh at or ridicule others for my friends.

7. I won't intentionally fail for my friends.

8. I won't behave irresponsibly for my friends.

9. I won't knowingly hurt others for my friends.

10. I won't destroy my life or anyone else's for my friends.

Anyone who would ask me to do any of these things, is not my friend.

Classroom

1. Clearly define, verbally affirm, and visually display your classroom vision, Code of Conduct, expectations, values, and beliefs.

2. Develop a consistent set of classroom procedures, rewards, and consequences to reinforce the values and beliefs including, but not limited to:

   - procedures for beginning and ending class.

   - procedures for quieting the classroom.

   - procedures for participating in classroom discussions.

   - procedures for facilitating and participating in group discussions.

   - consequences for unacceptable classroom language and behaviors.

   - procedures for missing school or turning in late assignments.

   - procedures for extra credit and making up assignments or tests.

- regular and effective parent communication of student behavior, student assignments, standardized testing dates, classroom tests, homework, and other areas to ensure the highest academic achievement levels.

3. Foster student collaboration through effective grouping of students, e.g., personality types, Multiple Intelligences, and learning styles, to help communicate and reinforce the values and beliefs of the classroom.

4. Establish individual and classroom achievement goals at the beginning of each grading period and foster a culture of collaboration and cooperation where students help each other.

5. Never grade on a curve. Inspire all students to aspire to become top performers.

My wife and I have developed a household culture of high academic achievement. We teach our sons that they are supposed to do as well as they are capable of doing and that they can only achieve their highest level of success by reading, studying, preparing for tests, and completing their schoolwork. We tell them that school is their "J-O-B." We expect them to get A's if they are capable of getting A's. We expect them to do their homework and we work to prepare them to do well on tests. We do not believe that boys, in general, or African-American children in particular, are less capable or less able to do well in school. We believe that developing your mind is like developing any other muscle in your body—you must stretch and work it. The weakest and smallest biceps can be developed and shaped through regular exercise, the correct diet, and proper nutrition.

As a parent, can you guarantee that your child will get a teacher who believes that he or she is capable of the very highest level of academic achievement? Of course not. However, it is in the best interest of your child to develop a relationship with his or her teachers, and to continually communicate to teachers that *you* expect the highest level of academic achievement your child is capable of. For some teachers you will have to be more specific: "I believe my child is capable of getting A's. Equally important is that my child be in a classroom setting that is emotionally nurturing." Anything you can do to help your child's teacher and your child's school foster a positive and supportive school climate and culture is in the best interest of your child.

Talk to other parents

Talk to as many parents as you can and ask for their opinions about the teachers in your child's school. Keep in mind that a great teacher for their child may not be a great teacher for your child. Also, the most popular teachers are not necessarily the best teachers. Consider other people's opinions as just that—opinions. Do not be quick to judge any teacher by what others say. You owe it to the teacher and you owe it to your child to sit and meet with the teacher. I am not interested in the most popular teacher or the teacher with the most advanced degrees or the teacher with the most teaching experience. I am interested in the person who can effectively teach my child and who will help my child to be successful and have positive experiences in his or her classroom.

When our son, Jalani, was in preschool, we moved him from one classroom into another classroom. My wife and I, despite our efforts, were unable to help his teacher understand how to effectively manage the 12 children in her classroom. We had Jalani moved into Mrs. Lake's classroom, despite the fact that Mrs. Lake already had 27 children in her classroom. What was most important to us was that Mrs. Lake was eager to work with us to help our son to have a successful school year.

Jalani did not want to go into her classroom. Every day he would say that it was time to go back to his old classroom. He did not like his new teacher; "Mrs. Lake is mean!" he would say. What Jalani did not like, was that Mrs. Lake would not allow him to get away with the behaviors he had been exhibiting in his previous classroom. Mrs. Lake would not send him to time-out, she would say, "Jalani I am going to call your mom and dad."

Despite Jalani's protests, he went on to have a wonderful year. Through our working in partnership with his teacher, he began to have more good days than bad ones. Although she had twice as many students, Mrs. Lake had a very well-managed classroom where some of the most difficult students in the school (our son included) learned to work together, play together, and achieve together.

Talking to other parents is not only therapeutic but provides the opportunity to, through the experiences of other parents, develop strategies unique to a child's development (e.g., high school versus middle school), gender (e.g., middle school-age boys), socioeconomic influences (e.g., urban street gangs versus suburban access to alcohol and drugs), or school culture (unwritten rules limiting student access to certain classes or extracurricular activities).

Parents have tremendous power to positively influence a school community by sharing their experiences and working together on behalf of their children and their children's school.

Questions to raise with your child's principal

In the meeting with your child's principal, you may consider asking some of the following questions:

- What is the school's mission and vision? What are your academic or standardized testing goals? What type of school climate and culture are you trying to cultivate and is there anything I can do as a parent to assist in your efforts?

- Have any teachers been recognized as "Teacher of the Year" or received national certification?

- Have any teachers published papers, written books, have specialized areas of expertise, or presented workshops?

- Are any teachers mentor or demonstration teachers?

- Do any teachers have professional experience in their subject area?

- Have teachers received awards, special recognition, or developed special programs?

- Is office referral, suspension, or discipline data available by grade level or by classroom?

- Are standardized test scores available by grade level and/or by classroom?

- Based on my child's personality type, learning style, multiple intelligences, and interests, are there teachers who you believe would be most effective with my child?

- Based on my child's interests and abilities are there programs, clubs, or activities you would recommend?

While I have stated it before, let me state again, "Be careful not to pre-judge any teacher." Some great teachers do not have high test scores because they get the most challenging students, which could also mean they have more office referrals or suspensions. Also, do not rush to judgment because of a teacher's years of experience. Some first-year teachers have been the best for our children in that they have been innovative, willing to listen, willing to learn, and eager to form a parent-teacher partnership. While some of the "experienced" teachers have been great also, we have encountered teachers who were "set in their ways," felt that the classroom was under their dictatorship, and refused to listen to parents or accept any parental input.

My experience is that principals at schools that are child-centered are eager to discuss their mission/vision, welcome the opportunity to talk to parents about the achievements of their teachers, readily share the discipline and achievement data of their school, and seek every opportunity to provide the best match of teachers and students to ensure the success for all.

Questions to raise with your child's teacher

After you have gathered your data, create a list of questions for each prospective teacher:

1. Considering my son's learning style how will you best help him to be successful in your classroom?

2. How much of my son's grade will be based on classroom participation or group work?

3. Will you do any Multiple Intelligences activities or will you allow my son any opportunities to present his work in a project through which he utilizes his

dominant intelligences (e.g., a dramatic presentation, writing a play, creating a model, making a group presentation, etc.)?

4. Do you plan to group your students? If so, will you take into consideration such things as personality types, learning styles, or multiple intelligences?

5. Do you allow students to make up assignments or re-take tests?

6. What is your discipline policy?

7. What is your grading policy and do you provide parent-friendly rubrics for major assignments?

    [Note: a rubric outlines specifically how an assignment will be graded and clearly outlines what is expected.]

8. What method do you use to keep parents informed of whether or not class work is being completed in class or homework is being turned in on time?

9. Do you notify parents of test dates and missing assignments? If so, how?

10. What types of things would you suggest that I do to ensure that my child has every opportunity to be successful in your classroom?

While teachers are not accustomed to parents raising these types of questions I have been pleasantly surprised to discover not only that many teachers welcome such questions, but that some teachers are prepared for such questions.

When our older son was attending the John Hopkins Middle School for the Arts and Communication Studies in St. Petersburg, Florida, his seventh-grade science teacher, Mrs. Haugabrook, not only welcomed such questions, she was prepared for these questions and more. While our son has been blessed to have had many good teachers during his years in school, Mrs. Haugabrook, qualifies as a "Great" teacher.

Among her many credits, Mrs. Haugabrook:
- *provided a study packet of helpful hints for note taking, time management, and organizational skills.*
- *provided parents with a brochure outlining her vision, discipline policy, grading philosophy, and expectations.*
- *had a web page where she posted assignments, lectures, and test dates.*
- *provided a voice mail number for weekly assignments.*
- *provided a clear rubric for all major assignments.*

- *provided a monthly calendar of assignments, lectures, and tests.*

- *provided the times and telephone numbers where she could be contacted during the day and during the evening.*

- *provided regular progress reports.*

- *was willing to initial our son's student agenda each day to indicate that he had turned in his homework.*

Needless to say, our son was not only an 'A' student in Mrs. Haugabrook's class but he was more excited about learning science than he had ever been about any subject other than art.

Whatever questions you raise with your child's teacher should be designed to open meaningful dialogue between parent and teacher. Developing a strong parent-teacher partnership will help to provide your child with every opportunity to succeed in school.

Assessing your child's school

While many parents do not have a choice of their public school, you should still assess the school before your child goes there. You must ask, "What can I do to help my child's school?" The best way to do a quick assessment of your child's school is to simply look and listen.

Go to your child's school at various times during the school day (i.e., in the morning, at lunch time, when students are changing classes, and when school is being dismissed). Observe the relationships between students and adults, observe how students are interacting with each other throughout the school community, and observe the behavior and enthusiasm of students in classrooms.

What is the school's mission/vision?

The first thing to look for is the school's mission/vision. Most school's have a mission statement posted in the front office. Less common is a vision statement. The mission of a school generally states what it wants to achieve, e.g., "educate children." The vision would incorporate and articulate the major beliefs of the school community. It guides the school toward achieving the mission, e.g., high academic achievement, positive social interactions, a safe school community, and/or parent-teacher partnerships. While the "School Improvement Plan" may provide specifics, it only supports the school's vision.

When our older son was attending Mt. Bethel Elementary School, in Marietta, Georgia, my wife and I got involved in helping the school to revise its vision. While the vision directed the school toward fostering a safe school community, helping children to achieve their academic, social, and personal potential, it did not say anything about dreams. We believe that a school should inspire children to discover and pursue their dreams and aspirations.

The school's vision was eventually re-written to incorporate the wording, "We believe that our students should have dreams and aspirations that will lead them into higher levels of learning." The following year's theme was, "Follow the Dream."

This vision, in part, led Mt. Bethel Elementary to become a Georgia Public Charter School so that the school could engage children in programs to further expose them to discovering, developing, defining, and pursuing their dreams and aspirations.

Things to look for

- What is the school's mission/vision and where is it posted?

- What messages do the visual images posted throughout the school communicate and celebrate (e.g., the diversity of the student population, career/college possibilities, academic achievement expectations, athletic or performance-related achievement expectations, teacher-staff achievements, community-business partnerships, parent involvement, student work, the school's values and beliefs, etc.)?

- Beginning with the opening bell, observe students and staff interactions; in the main office; in corridors; in classrooms; in the cafeteria; in the library; and outside of the school.

- Observe student behaviors within classrooms. Do students appear to be approaching their studies with a sense of passion and purpose or is there apathy and disinterest?

- Are there photographs of students, staff, parents, and community persons interacting or engaging in student-centered programs and activities?

- Are there bulletin boards that celebrate themes and promote high expectations and learning outcomes?

- Are the corridors and bathrooms clean?

- Is the front office organized?

- Do teachers dress professionally?

Visual images capture the synergy and reveal the culture of a school. What you see provides a glimpse into the attitudes, behaviors, and beliefs of people throughout the school community. As a parent, this exercise can sensitize you to some of the issues that will ultimately affect your child.

Things to listen for

- Is there yelling and screaming?

- Are students loud and rowdy?

- Do you hear profanity?

- Do you hear verbal put downs by teachers or students?

- Are students being encouraged to articulate, share, or discuss their opinions and ideas?

- Listen to how the office staff answers the telephone and greets visitors.

Of all of the things I listen for in a school, I pay particular attention to how teachers speak to students and whether or not they reinforce standard English usage in the classroom. Are students being encouraged to speak in complete sentences? For example, "The capital of Georgia is Atlanta. Two plus two equals four."

I have worked in schools where children frequently spoke in slang or incorrect grammar and teachers rarely corrected them: "I ain't got none. Don't be bothering me. I ain't got no paper," or "What that is?" Children in these schools were not being taught to speak in the language patterns in which they would be tested and which they would be responsible for using in their future jobs.

It is common for children to speak in cultural language patterns around family and friends, and in their communities outside of school that may depart from standard English usage or correct grammar. However, the responsibility of the school's staff and teachers is to teach and reinforce standard English usage.

Teachers must expect all students to learn correct grammar and to speak standard English in their classrooms. It is their job to model, teach, and consistently reinforce standard English usage. This is the only way they can effectively prepare students for the many standardized tests they will be given.

Go to the school during the year before your child begins school. Walk around the building and look into the classrooms for the grade that your child will be entering. Ask lots of questions:

- Are there any special clubs or organizations (e.g., chess, math, computer, science, foreign language, speech and debate, drama, etc.)?

- Are there special instructional programs in music, art, band, animation, cheer leading, athletics, etc?

- Do students work on the school newspaper, yearbook, produce television programs, or become involved in special interest groups or other types of extended learning opportunities?

- Are there before- or after-school programs?

- Does the school offer special test preparation classes?

- Does the school offer tutoring or mentoring?

- Does the school provide opportunities for students to compete in Quiz Bowls, Spelling Bees, Geography Bowls, cheer leading, chess, math, art, martial arts, or science competitions?

When our older son was in the seventh grade he was invited by his Social Studies teacher to join the Economics Quiz Bowl team representing his middle school. For several weeks he joined a group of seventh- and eighth-grade students who stayed after school twice a week to prepare to compete in the county-wide Middle School Economics Quiz Bowl competition.

His team went on to win the county-wide championship marking the first time that the arts magnet school had ever placed higher than fourth. Their victory culminated in a reception and awards presentation by the Superintendent of Schools.

After gathering your information, it is time to prepare a plan for each of your children.

Teacher Strategies

- Develop a consistent set of classroom procedures, rewards, and consequences to provide the foundation for school success (e.g., beginning/ending class, quieting the classroom, participating in classroom discussions, facilitating group discussions, submitting missing or late assignments).

- Provide regular and effective parent communication of student behavior, student assignments, standardized testing dates, classroom tests, homework, and other areas to ensure the highest academic achievement levels.

- Establish individual and classroom achievement goals at the beginning of each grading period and foster a culture of collaboration and cooperation where students help each other become successful.

- Look for opportunities to encourage student participation in activities and programs throughout the school community.

S tep 3

Develop a Plan

Now that you have gathered information about your child and your child's school, what is your plan? Simply, what do *you* want your child to learn, experience, and/or be exposed to this school year? (You cannot simply say, "I want my child to learn as much as he or she can!")

Be specific:

- Do you want your child to learn more math, science, reading, writing, social studies, art, music, or social skills?

- Do you want your child to learn computer graphics, computer programming, web page design, architecture, fashion design, cosmetology, culinary arts, or construction?

- Do you want your child to learn about the stock market, the Internet, investments, or entrepreneurship?

- Do you want your child to learn how to be more responsible?

- Do you want your child to learn how to be more independent?

- Do you want your child to learn how to become a better baseball, basketball, football, soccer, or tennis player?

- Do you want your child to learn how to become a better swimmer, dancer, singer, actor, artist, musician, or playwright?

- Do you want your child to be nurtured so that he or she can discover his or her gifts and talents?

- Do you want your child exposed to other people and cultures?

- Do you want your child to enroll into more honors, AP, or academically-gifted classes?

You must think about these and countless other things to put together your plan. Do not rely on the school to determine the complete scope of what your child needs to know. Use whatever they suggest as a guide. Keep in mind that the school's curriculum is geared toward helping students to achieve minimum proficiency standards established by the State Department of Education. Most students can soar beyond the minimum proficiency standards when we can tap their passion for learning. While some students may be ready to be introduced to addition, your child may be ready to be introduced to algebra. While some students may be ready to read chapter books, your child may be ready to read classic literature. While some students may be ready for grammar and sentence structure, your child may be ready for writing novels or publishing books of poetry.

Because of the plan that we put into place for our then, nine-year-old son, transferring from one of the highest academically achieving schools to a school for the arts, we believe that his needs were best served. He is about to graduate from high school and has been accepted into Amherst College (his first-choice school). While attending the Pinellas County Schools elementary and middle school magnet program for the arts he received instruction by some of the country's best art teachers. Since he was in all advanced classes, his academic teachers, several of whom had national certification, were among the best middle school teachers any parent could hope for. In addition to high-level academic instruction he learned graphics and illustration computer software such as Adobe Photoshop, Adobe Illustrator, PageMaker, Microsoft Word, FreeHand, and QuarkXPress. All of these techniques and software applications are used by professional artists and full-time graphic artists.

He learned college-level shading and other artistic techniques, had his artwork professionally framed, displayed in art shows, and exhibited in the Salvador Dali Museum.

After relocating back to Georgia where he has attended North Springs High School, our plan was to ensure that he had an academically rigorous course schedule to make him a competitive candidate for college admissions. We ensured that his high school course schedule included honors, AP, advanced science and advanced math classes. Subsequently, our son will graduate having taken a total of 14 art, 11 honors, 7 AP, 5 math, and 5 science classes. He will receive the Dual Magnet Seal of Distinction for Visual & Performing Arts and Math & Science.

Our younger son has done well academically in each school and school district he has attended. Currently in middle school, he has become an all-star athlete, honor roll student, and has demonstrated great talent in acting and singing. His middle school plan has him on track to take Spanish and Algebra I for high school credit. A further focus on preparing him for standardized testing and providing the necessary at-home support to help him to qualify for the honor roll each grading period during middle school will further help him to qualify for advanced math and science classes when he enters high school.

David Conley, in <u>College Knowledge: What High School Students Know About College Readiness</u>, notes:

The most single most important factor in determining college success is the academic challenge of the courses students take in high school. This is particularly true for students from racial and ethnic minority groups. African-American and Latino students' college degree completion rates are more positively affected than that of any other group by a high-quality, academically intense high school curriculum.

The subject in the curriculum that is most predictive of college success is the level of mathematics completed.

What is your vision?

While reading, writing, and arithmetic are undeniably important, you must ask, "What are my child's special gifts, interests, dreams and aspirations?" Answering these question will help you develop a plan based upon the unique needs and gifts of your child. There is a verse of scripture that reads, *"Where there is no vision, the people perish,"* *[Proverbs 19:18]*. Do you want your child to perish in school? To attend school each day without passion and purpose or without dreams and aspirations? Without a future or destination? Of course not. But this is exactly the way millions of children leave home each day to enter school. We have been so busy focusing on the behaviors, attitudes, grades, and test scores of the present that we have not taken the time to help children focus on the potential and possibilities of the future.

Begin with the end in mind! Focus on the wonderful, magnificent, intelligent, educated person you see your child becoming and work backwards. For example, if you see your child becoming a doctor, then help her to walk, speak, and behave responsibly like a doctor, today. Help her to begin developing the character of a good doctor, today. Begin using and spelling medical terms at home, today. Get your preschooler a doctor's kit. Get your elementary child a medical dictionary and encyclopedia. Get your middle school child a microscope and a listing of medical schools. Familiarize your high school student with college applications and admissions requirements as he or she enters high school. Your daughter should know the test scores, grades, and student activities which will best prepare her to compete for admission into the colleges which will best prepare her to enter into the medical school of her choice. Now is the time to focus on qualifying for a college scholarship.

Mrs. Lessie Hamilton-Rose, principal of Flower City School in Rochester, New York, gives her elementary school students a college-bound vision. Mrs. Rose arranges a field trip for her fourth- and fifth-grade students to a local college each school year. She started a college scholarship fund that any Flower City Student is eligible for when he or she graduates from high school and is accepted into a college or university.

I was working with children at an elementary school when one of the teachers asked if I would speak to Brittany. "Mr. Wynn, will you talk to Brittany? Brittany is an evil child! She always talks about people and is always fighting and getting into trouble."

I invited Brittany to join me for lunch. Brittany came into the cafeteria with five other little girls. Brittany and her little friends strutted into the cafeteria as though they were in charge and they were not to be messed with!

As Brittany and the other little girls sat down at the table, I began talking about my family. I shared with them what our dreams were. I told them about my wife and my children. I went on to ask each of the girls what their dreams were. Without hesitation Brittany said, "Mr. Wynn, I want to be a doctor." I asked, "What type of doctor would you like to become, Brittany?" Again, without hesitation, Brittany said, "A pediatrician." One of the other little girls at the table said, "What type of doctor is that?" Brittany responded, "A baby doctor, fool!"

This was my opportunity to "connect" Brittany's long-term dreams with her current behavior. "Brittany, is that the way you would speak to one of your patients if they had a question regarding your diagnosis?" Brittany thought for a moment and looked at the little girl, "That's a baby doctor. Okay?"

After our delightful lunch, each of the little girls left affirming their dreams and aspirations. Brittany got up from the table, threw her trash away, waved good-bye, and walked away with her head held high. She walked away with the confidence that she could, in fact, become a doctor.

I went on to share my delightful lunch experience with the teacher who had asked that I speak to Brittany. "Did you know that Brittany wants to become a doctor?" The teacher immediately responded, "Well, Brittany is retarded, Mr. Wynn!"

Look beyond the labels to the gifts

Within many school communities children are defined by labels—Mentally Handicapped, Learning Disabled, Emotionally Disturbed, Behavioral Disorder, or Attention Deficit Disorder. Many parents reaffirm such labels:

"My son is hyperactive."

"My daughter is LD."

"My son is not doing well in school because he is ADD."

We must never forget that children are God's work-in-progress, continually being perfected. We must be particularly careful not to allow labels to determine the scope of our dreams or influence the amount of thought and effort we put into developing the plans for our children. We must never stop looking for the interests, gifts, potential and possibilities in children.

Whatever you and your child dream of gives you a long-term focus. Current attitudes, behaviors, language, and achievement levels should become consistent with traveling along the road to achieving those long-term dreams and aspirations.

You do not have to have a perfect plan. You will adjust your plan many times as your child's interests, dreams, and aspirations change. As you talk to more people and gather more information, you will continually define and re-define your plan. As you witness the learning outcomes of your child in each school year, you will adjust and expand your plan.

Perhaps the most important components of your plan will be to continually expose your child to new opportunities and experiences and to help your child experience success each school year. Good grades, high test scores, positive experiences, and opportunities to expand and share his or her interests will all provide your child with the feeling of success; the feeling of being capable.

Make it a point to celebrate each of your children's successes. Post awards around your home. Take pictures of your children engaging in their interests. The more each of your children feels successful the more they will be successful. Never forget that whatever your children's interests, make reading a part of the process. Parents are often so excited about their child playing a sport, a musical instrument, or engaging in some other type of activity they forget about the importance of reading. Learning how to read is not an option. Do not allow a day to pass that your child does not read. Begin the day with breakfast and end the day with a book. The ability to read and to understand what he or she has read is one of the keys to success. As parents of boys, my wife and I are well aware of the resistance that many boys demonstrate when it comes to reading. However, if you want to ensure that your son gets onto the fast track to academic achievement ensure that he has more books than he does video games and that he spends more time reading than he does playing video games!

The rules in our home are:

1. No video game playing during the school week.

2. No video game playing on the weekends prior to all homework being completed and tests and quizzes studied for.

3. You must maintain a two to one ratio of reading to video game playing, i.e., read for one hour entitles you to play a video game for half an hour, read for two hours entitles you to play a video game for an hour, etc.

4. Violate any of the rules and you forfeit your video game playing time until the holiday break or end of the school year.

Look for the right teacher

I want my son to be in the classroom with a teacher who wants to help him feel successful. My son may not be successful on the first assignment or on the first test. I want a teacher who will allow for, and encourage him to resubmit papers, re-do assignments or re-take tests, over and over and over again until he can become successful. Even when the teacher does not allow our son to receive credit for re-doing an assignment we appreciate teachers who will at least accept the assignment as a means of motivating our son to continue trying. Learning, like parenting, is a marathon—not a sprint. Our children must learn how to apply themselves until they can achieve the level of success they are capable of achieving. Winning is not as important as realizing one's potential.

A good friend of mine, Dee Blassie, is the type of teacher I wish my children could have each year. She is always learning and growing, a continuing work in progress. Dee posts huge letters in her classroom that read, "Welcome to Success." She asks children repeatedly throughout the school year, "Honey, tell me how Mrs. Blassie can help you to become more successful?" She fosters parent partnerships, alumni partnerships, and business and mentoring partnerships. Dee does anything that she can to help expose her students to life's wonderful opportunities. Her classroom is a warm, engaging, nurturing environment for children. She is concerned each year with the dreams and aspirations of her students. She is less concerned with where they come from and more concerned with where they can go with the education that she inspires them to reach for.

If you believe that a teacher, subject, program, camp or other opportunity would be best for your child, write it down and make it a part of your plan. Always look for opportunities to develop your child physically, intellectually, socially, and artistically. Some parents push their children exclusively toward sports. Others push their children exclusively toward academic achievement. Others want their children to wear the latest clothing styles and be popular socially. It is important for you to provide opportunities for your child to pursue his or her passions and areas of interest, however, you must help your child to become well-rounded and it is your job to ensure that your child is learning. Cute is good, but critical thinking is better. Dunking a basketball is good, but dunking the SAT is better. Throwing a football is good, but throwing a business plan together is better. Wearing the latest styles is good, but wearing straight A's is better.

Whatever talents, abilities, or interests your son or daughter has you must evaluate what he of she wants to do with what you want him or her to do and stay focused on your plan. You are the parent and you are responsible for preparing your son or daughter to become successful. As my niece would say, "If you don't know, you'd better ask somebody!"

Special connections

If your daughter talks a lot, try to get her involved in drama, speech and debate, broadcast journalism, law or other programs to develop her oratory skills. If she likes to draw or is very creative, find a program that will help her to further develop her artistic skills. If she has a passion for problem-solving expose her to a program that will further develop her computational and problem-solving abilities. Review the Multiple Intelligences areas that you identified and ask yourself, "What future opportunities could my daughter pursue in the areas where she has demonstrated an interest, talent, or ability?" Discovering the right areas of interest for your child could make all of the difference in how he or she feels about school. Helping your child to develop a passion for learning and fostering a sense of purpose could make school a wonderful and exciting place.

If there are clubs, summer camps, or other opportunities that have special requirements, make sure you know what they are. For example, to join the band you may need one year of music instruction or joining the math club may require a certain grade in math and a certain overall grade point average.

Talk about the clubs, special interest activities, and classes offered at the school with your child to see what he or she may be interested in. Keep in mind that YOU must make the final decision. Your child may be talented in an area which could qualify him or her for a college scholarship, however, he or she may be more interested in socializing with friends rather than studying, practicing, or spending the necessary amount of time to further develop his or her gifts and abilities. During middle school, our older son wanted to take a guitar class, however, we made the decision to put him into graphic arts! He wanted to play baseball after school. We said okay, however, he had to join the staff of the school magazine after school also. There he would learn even more about graphic arts, layout, and design. Do not forget that you are the parent. It is your job to make decisions in the best interest of your child. You must balance what your child wants to do with what you believe he or she needs to do.

Each school year you must decide what you want your child to know, what sports or activities you want your child to participate in, and what programs, opportunities, and people you would like your child to be exposed to. While some children will eagerly provide you with a list of programs, camps, or sports they want to participate in, other children will require that you are more hands on in guiding their way.

Organize your plan into the following areas:

1.   Long-term dreams and aspirations: e.g., family; career; travel; special skills; exposure; politics; entrepreneurship, etc.

2.   Short- and long-term goals: e.g., honor roll; National Honor Society; advanced or honors classes; standardized test scores; college; becoming proficient in a foreign language; academic or athletic scholarships; art, music or other type of special instruction, etc.

3.   Things you would like for your child to learn or be exposed to.

4.   Ways in which you would like your child to grow personally: e.g., become more responsible; develop better study habits; increase his or her math scores; become more organized, etc.

5.   Clubs, extracurricular, special interest, special programs, or after-school activities you would like your child to experience.

6. Classes, coursework, extracurricular activities, and community service that will make your child a competitive candidate for college admissions.

   When planning for college, keep in mind that the requirements for admissions into state universities, out-of-state public universities, private universities, and junior or community colleges will vary widely. So too, with the cost of tuition, room, and board.

7. Refer to the books, *A Middle School Plan for Students with College-Bound Dreams*, and *A High School Plan for Students with College-Bound Dreams* to ensure that your child is on track to take the most rigorous classes that he or she is capable of succeeding in.

Teacher Strategies

- Demonstrate an interest in student success by recommending programs, extracurricular activities, enrichment opportunities, summer camps, tutoring, after-school programs, and classes.

- Recognize unique student talents in completing coursework and class participation, e.g., art, public speaking, problem-solving, etc.

- Assist students/families in identifying available information in formulating k-12 course schedules based on student gifts, interests, and aspirations.

S tep 4

Meet the Staff

You have prepared information about your child. You have gathered information about the school. You have a plan. Now what?

Contact the school and request a meeting with the principal and/or counselor. Prior to the meeting, give them a copy of your plan and the background information pertaining to your child (e.g., learning style, Multiple Intelligences, best learning situations, personality type, etc.). The purpose of this meeting is to ask the principal and/or counselor for their input as to how the school can best help you to help your child to become successful. How you prepare for this meeting will help to shape their perceptions about you as a parent. Keep in mind that this meeting is about relationship building. You want to develop a relationship, and shape perceptions, that says:

1. I am concerned about my child's success in school.

2. I have invested time gathering information that will be helpful in the placement of my child.

3. I want to be an involved parent.

4. I want to develop an effective parent-teacher and parent-school partnership.

5. I have expectations of what I would like for my child to learn and the type of teacher(s) who could best help my child.

Keep in mind that the principal wants high academic achievement, low absenteeism, and few office referrals and suspensions. By providing the principal with the information that you have regarding your child, the right placement can help the principal achieve his or her goals, and can help you achieve yours.

When you enter the school

When you enter the front office, meet, greet, and shake hands with all of the office staff. As soon as possible, write down the names of each person in the front office, however, do not stop there. Get to know as many of the people in the school as possible—cafeteria workers, custodians, coaches, administrators, safety officers, and the school bus driver.

My wife and I try to develop relationships with all of the adults who are there to look out for and look after our sons. I have found that the custodians and safety officers at the high school and cafeteria workers in the elementary school know a lot about what is going on in the school and what our children are doing when they are not around us.

At the meeting with the principal and/or counselor, discuss the information you have gathered about your child and ask, "How can you help place my child with a teacher or team of teachers who can provide the best learning environment for my child?"

At this meeting, let the principal and/or counselor know what your expectations are for your child and what types of activities you would like your child to participate in. Ask if there is anything else that he or she needs to know about your child to assist in class placement.

When we relocated back to Georgia, from Florida, our younger son was in the first grade. There were only six weeks left in the school year. To help in our transition we asked Dr. Brown, the school's principal, if our son could be placed into Mrs. Mabary's classroom. We did not care if another teacher had fewer students. Mrs. Mabary was our older son's first-grade teacher before we moved to Florida. She had excellent classroom management and never had to send children to time-out. In fact, when our son came home from school his first day he proclaimed, "Dad, Mrs. Mabary does not have time-out in her classroom. No one acts badly in her classroom." The principal, Dr. Brown, and Mrs. Mabary helped to ensure that our son made a successful transition into a new school setting.

Similarly, our older son entered into the seventh grade. Again, with only six weeks left in the school year. The seventh-grade counselor not only thoughtfully established a class schedule that helped to reduce the stress of entering into a new curriculum and new school setting so late into the school year, she assigned our son to an academic team where he already had friends whom he had previously attended elementary school with. She also arranged for his best friend to be his guide for the first day of school. This helped our son to make both a smooth academic and social transition into his new middle school.

Walk with the principal into the classrooms for the grade level your child will be entering. Notice how the teacher and students are interacting in each classroom and how they respond to you and the principal as you enter the room.

If your child has special needs, ask the principal to introduce you to the special education teachers, counselor, psychologist, school nurse or other special needs persons. If your child has any special interests in areas like art, music, or foreign languages, ask the principal to introduce you to those teachers. As you walk through the school with the principal and as you meet the teachers, keep in mind that this is going to be your child's school. Not *their* school but *your* school.

Ask the principal for any information that would be helpful—the school's newsletter, PTA information, School Advisory Council information, School Improvement Plan, special programs, discipline policy, sports and other extracurricular activities, etc.

Once your child is assigned to a classroom, schedule a conference with each of your child's teachers. Oftentimes, parents of elementary school students will know the classroom teacher but never talk to the P.E., art, music, or other rotational or subject-area teachers (e.g., science, math, foreign language, etc.). If you cannot schedule a conference send a note to each of your child's teachers as quickly as possible and share with them information about your child and the best way to contact you. Give your entire package of information to your child's classroom or homeroom teacher and let the teachers know that you want to work with them in whatever way possible to ensure your child has a successful school year.

Develop relationships

Keep in mind that all of this is relationship building. Whenever you receive a note from teachers relating to your child's behavior, classroom participation, or schoolwork, ask, "What would you suggest that I do?" You can always refer to the information that you provided for clues as to whether the problem is in your child's attitudes and behaviors, in the relationship with the teacher, in the way information is being presented within the classroom, in the dynamics of the classroom, or related to peer pressures. Whatever the problem, stay focused on your vision, "To help your child to be successful in school." The relationships you develop through your initial contact with teachers is the foundation of the parent-teacher partnership needed to ensure your child's success in school.

The family serves as the social vehicle through which a child's natural genius can be activated and realized in the world. It does this by providing an atmosphere that nourishes children's inner gifts and talents. There are specific features present in all positive family climates that help to accomplish this goal, including the cultivation of active learning, positive values, nurturing relationships, and self-esteem.

[Awakening Your Child's Natural Genius]

Teacher Strategies

Step 1: Engage students in an exploratory activity (e.g., personal essay, illustration, interdisciplinary unit, college-planning discussion) related to their goals, dreams, or college-career aspirations.

Step 2: Attach the exploratory activity to the course syllabus or welcome letter requesting the preferred means of contacting parents/guardians (e.g., face-to-face, email, note, telephone).

Step 3: Communicate your vision for student success, supply requests, parent involvement activities, and a checklist of what parents would feel most comfortable contributing.

Step 4: Commit to a parent-teacher partnership in student social development and academic success.

Step 5: Identify students most at risk and identify people within the school community to become part of their "web of protection."

All I Really Need to Know I Learned in Kindergarten
by Robert Fulghum

- Share everything
- Play fair
- Don't hit people
- Put things back where you found them
- Clean up your own mess
- Don't take things that aren't yours
- Say you're sorry when you hurt somebody
- Wash your hands before you eat
- Flush
- Warm cookies and cold milk are good for you
- Live a balanced life—learn some and think some and draw and paint and sing and dance and play and work every day some
- Take a nap every afternoon
- When you go out in the world, watch out for traffic, hold hands and stick together
- Be aware of wonder. Remember the little seed in the Styrofoam cup: the roots go down and the plant goes up and nobody really knows how or why, but we are all like that.
- Goldfish and hamsters and white mice and even the little seed in the Styrofoam cup—they all die. So do we.
- And then remember the Dick-and-Jane books and the first word you learned—the biggest word of all—LOOK

No matter how old you are, when you go out in the world, it is best to hold hands and stick together.

Step 5

Be Visible

Beginning with the first day of school, go to your child's school as often as you can. Just show up and walk around. Remember, this is your school. Find out what the school's policy is for visiting classrooms. Follow the policy and visit your child's classrooms.

Be sure to meet and greet the principal, teachers, and office staff by name. If you have a hard time remembering names, make notes about each person and associate their names with physical features. "Mr. Jones, tall! Ms. Smith, red hair. Mrs. Johnson, reminds me of my mother!"

Let your child know that you may show up any time and unannounced. Look in on him or her and observe the classroom dynamics and your child's participation. Elementary school students love for parents to come to their classroom or to have lunch with them. Middle school students *hate* for parents to come to their school. High school students *want to die* whenever their parent comes to their school. Remember, you are the parent and you are responsible for doing what is in the best interest of your child. From my experiences of being involved in hundreds of middle and high schools throughout America; one of the biggest problems is the absence of parents. The behaviors of students and staff alike are positively affected by parents being in the building. The best thing that could happen to create safer and higher academically achieving middle and high schools would be for parents to become involved on a day-to-day basis in schools. This truly would be a rebirth of the village.

If you can, go to PTA/PTSA meetings, performances, workshops, or other meetings held at the school. Take advantage of any opportunity to get involved in the school. Even if your schedule does not permit you to attend all of the school meetings and functions it is important for teachers to see you around the school. You want them to know that you care about your child's education.

If you cannot attend the meetings at the school, try to get to know other parents and talk to them after the meetings so that you can stay informed. Whenever you attend functions at the school and meet other parents take advantage of the opportunity to exchange telephone numbers and/or e-mail addresses.

I [Marva Collins] believe that the classroom of every American school must become the flame that will enlighten the world, fire the imagination, give might to dreams and wings to the aspirations of girls and boys so that they may dare to become literate citizens of their locales, and with equal comfortableness, citizens of the universe.

["Ordinary" Children, Extraordinary Teachers]

Even if you cannot regularly attend PTA/PTSA meetings you **must** volunteer to do something at your child's school. Think of what you do well, what you like to do, or what you are interested in doing and volunteer to do that at your child's school. Cooking, arts and crafts, helping to decorate or maintain bulletin boards, building cabinets, taking photographs, landscaping, gardening, quilting, storytelling, filing books in the library, reading to children, helping children on special projects, helping out in the classroom, helping out in the school office, chaperoning a field trip, or helping out at special events. There are opportunities to join the School Advisory Council, booster clubs, or to assist with the School Improvement Plan. Do anything to get involved, to support your child's school and to help the people who are helping your child.

If you cannot go to the school during the week, try to volunteer to help at weekend or after-school programs. You can volunteer to do things at home in the evenings. Teachers have many projects they work on at home that you can help with. If you can, take off from work and stop by the school in the mornings or afternoons. If you cannot volunteer time then donate something. Books, school supplies, videos, audio tapes, tape recorders, computers, clothes, or anything to help the school better serve the needs of children and families.

My wife and I have volunteered at our sons' elementary, middle, and high school. We have worked with administrators to develop the school's vision. We have cut out "feet" at home in the evening for our son's elementary school. My wife and a friend started a Spanish language program at the school. I volunteered one weekend to run cable and telephone wire throughout the school to connect classrooms to the Internet. We have volunteered to help with field days, field trips, school opening, and planning meetings with teachers. At our older son's high school we worked with the football booster club and athletic association. My wife and I took pictures during football, lacrosse, and track and field seasons and posted them to the school's web site and onto a bulletin board at the entrance to the school.

If you cannot volunteer, maybe someone from your church, sorority, or fraternity, or a grandparent, co-worker, or neighbor can volunteer on your behalf. Schools typically qualify for additional funding based on the total number of volunteer hours. Explore the opportunities of getting your company to become a business partner with your child's school or to donate office equipment, supplies, or expertise.

If you cannot go to your child's school then stay visible and involved through notes to your child's teacher and principal. If you come across interesting newspaper or magazine articles, or books, get a copy and send them to the teacher with a note, "I thought you may be interested in this." Share this book with your child's teacher as a means of exchanging thoughts and ideas regarding the issues being raised. If the principal and teachers at your child's school are connected to the Internet, share your ideas with them via e-mail.

Get an inspirational note pad or note cards and send questions or comments regarding your child's schoolwork to his or her teacher. Whenever your child has difficulty with an assignment or test, review your child's learning style and talk to the teacher to see if there is anything that can be done to help your child better understand the information and concepts being covered in class.

Go to the parent-teacher conferences or send someone on your behalf. Demonstrate an interest in, and be aware of, what your child is doing in school and whether or not he or she is understanding and learning what is being taught.

Teacher Strategies

Step 1: Clearly communicate your mission/vision for student success within your classroom and/or program.

Step 2: Create a checklist of parent involvement opportunities, e.g., booster club, event preparation, assisting with experiments, field trips, photography, videography, tutoring assistance, monitoring make-up tests, writing newsletters, college visits, guest speakers.

Step 3: With a continual focus on "What's in the best interests of students" make parents partners in creating a learning culture.

Step 4: Provide frequent informal opportunities for cultivating parent-parent relationships and developing parent planning teams.

Step 5: Provide formal methods of recognizing parent support, e.g., certificates, pins, trophies, T-shirts, etc.

S tep 6

Tell Teachers How to Best Communicate With You

It is important to have good communication with your child's teachers. Let teachers know what you expect in terms of behavior, classroom participation, homework, class work, and grades. Ask each teacher for suggestions about the best way for the two of you to keep in touch. It is important for the teacher to know that you want to be involved and that you want the teacher to contact you whenever there is a problem.

Some teachers do not make parents aware of behavioral problems, learning problems, or missed assignments until it is time for grades. It is too late to do anything about it then! You can avoid such situations by making it clear to teachers that you want to be informed of any problems, e.g., missed assignments, failure to turn in homework, poor test/quiz preparation, not paying attention in class, etc., as soon as a problem occurs.

You and your child's teachers must agree on a primary communication method. If you want your child's teachers to call, tell them when, where, and at what time. If you want them to send notes home, tell them what you need them to do to double check that your child gives you the note! In some cases, it may require that you sign and return the note or write your response in your child's agenda. Be sure to give teachers a copy of your signature at the beginning of the school year. Do not be so naive as to believe that your little "angel" would never forge your signature!

My son's preschool teacher was having a problem with her sixth-grader's behavior in class. His teacher usually had to tell him over and over and over again to perform certain tasks or to complete his class work. His mother was not made aware of this problem until she received his first report card. By then a pattern of behavior had developed between both the teacher and her son. I suggested that she have his teacher send a note home each day with a tally of how many times she had to repeat herself when giving him instructions in the classroom throughout the day.

The first day that his mother received the note from his teacher it read: "I had to tell Robert to put away his things eight times. I had to tell Robert to complete his math six times ..."

Robert had to go to bed five minutes early for each time that his teacher had to repeat her instructions. The next day Robert followed his teacher's instructions the first time all day!

This is a perfect example of why effective communication is one of the keys to your child's success in school. If your child needs a little "push" to ensure that he or she studies for tests and quizzes, tell your child's teacher to send a note home to let you know well in advance of quizzes or tests. Ask her to send a rubric or study guide so you can ensure your child studies the correct material and so you can pretest your child on the material being covered.

Your method of communication may vary by school and/or by teacher. We used a folder with a monthly calendar and e-mail during elementary school, the student agenda and e-mail during middle school, and our school district's online system, "Parent Connect" and e-mail during high school. In the case of those teachers who were slow to respond to our e-mails we discovered that when we copied the principal on our e-mail, they generally responded promptly.

After continual and ongoing communication to, and collaboration with, our younger son's elementary school teachers we received an e-mail from his then, fifth-grade teacher.

My, what a journey this has been!!!!!!

Teachers who know of Jalani (but have never taught him) stopped me all day long to comment on how impressed they were with his performance today. What an awesome experience it has been for me to watch the little boy who ran around the front office transform into the confident kid on stage performing one of the lead roles in 'A Midsummer Night's Dream'!!!

Jalani was basking in the stage lights--clearly joyous about being on stage and having full permission to talk--dance, perform, and be a goofball, as well! Have you ever seen more of an advertisement for playing to an individual's learning style? Wow!!!!

I have always loved Jalani--you know I asked to have him in my class for fourth grade. This year has been fascinating for me because I have watched him grow into himself day by day. Mr. Wynn, you were right!!!!! I give you full credit--you know your kid, and you could predict the outcome of looping for Jalani--even as he was struggling with relationships last year.

Watching Jalani grow has been interesting because he seems to be developing different facets of who he is: the dedicated student alongside the kind, funny, and caring friend. He is taking responsibility in his academics while goofing off with buddies! What fun!!!!!! These are the qualities we all strive for ... discipline when necessary for career success, and compassion and humor when it comes to family and friends. It is a pleasure to watch him be-bop down the hall with a constant smile on his face now, too. No more sour puss as sometimes found in the past.

What a job you have done--allowing Jalani to be Jalani (and listening to his constant stream of words as he is continuing to grow into himself!!) Thank you for your support, always, and letting me witness and take part in this kid's life. As teachers, we aren't supposed to have favorites, but ... you've got two kids who are completely and totally unforgettable! Favorites who will never be forgotten--for being themselves and helping me to become a better teacher.

Happy Thanksgiving!

Our younger son, Jalani, is currently in the sixth grade and we continue our ongoing communication with his teachers through his student agenda and e-mail. In Step 2, *Identify the Best School,* I raised the issue of school climate and culture. School culture is clearly evident in the openness and willingness of teacher-parent communication. The entire sixth-grade team at our son's middle school is child-centered and parent-friendly. Communication is regular and ongoing and the tone of the communication is always, "What is in Jalani's best interest?" Effective home-school communication is particularly important at the transition points, i.e., elementary to middle school (usually sixth grade) and middle school to high school (usually ninth grade).

In order for any communication method to be effective, it must be consistently used. Many parents make the mistake of believing that communication with teachers is important during elementary school, less important during middle school, and unnecessary during high school. Nothing could be further from the truth! Parent-teacher communication is important to a child's school success from preschool through high school. Some children require infrequent communication while other children require regular and ongoing communication. However, all children require some measure of parent-teacher communication. As our older son enters the twelfth grade, this is the first year that we have not had ongoing communication with his teachers. We are allowing him some space as warranted by his level of maturity and personal responsibility. However, we still have open and regular communication with his principal, magnet coordinator, counselor, and school safety officers!

In the case of our younger son, we review his agenda daily, remind him of any failure to note assignments or test dates, and respond to teacher notes and/or comments. Middle school students have so many classes, so much class work, homework, and tests that parents need to communicate regularly with their child's teachers or a child can quickly fall behind. Some children fall so far behind that it is nearly impossible to catch up before the end of a grading period.

As parents, we want to know on a daily basis how our children are behaving so that we can work with them on any problem areas before they escalate into classroom disruptions, office referrals, or suspension from school.

At the end of the day, during fifth grade, our son was responsible for giving his agenda to his teacher and she simply wrote, "Good day," to let us know there were no problems with his behavior and he had completed and turned in all of his assignments. Mychal-David developed a habit of doing his homework only to bury it in his backpack or stuff it into his desk and not turn it in! This daily method of communication helped us to help him be successful in school until he became responsible about turning in his work (this process, with some adjustments, took us through eleventh grade before he became totally responsible for completing and turning in his schoolwork).

When our current middle schooler was in preschool, he had a monthly calendar (which we called a "Traffic Light Book") on which his teacher placed a green, yellow, or red sticker each day representing expected, less than expected, and unacceptable behavior. Each day when we picked him up from school we asked, "Jalani, what color sticker did you get today?" This system kept us informed each day of his classroom behavior.

Maintain high expectations

Take your child's grades seriously and let your child's teacher know that you take them seriously. Stereotypes abound in schools. Some teachers do not believe that minority children are capable of straight A's or high test scores. Other teachers do not believe that boys are capable of high grades or high test scores. Other teachers do not believe that girls can do well in math and science. Unfortunately, there are still teachers who do not believe that poor children are capable of high academic achievement.

It is important for you to continually, and without compromise, have the highest expectations of your child's academic performance. If your son or daughter is capable of getting A's then you should be relentless in your encouraging and affirming that he or she get A's. If your son or daughter is capable of scoring 100 percent on tests, then he or she should score 100 percent, and, if extra credit is offered he or she should do that as well. No matter what his or her ability level, only by working harder do children get smarter. The bright child who easily gets straight A's should be pushed to tutor other children, develop projects, build models, and apply themselves far beyond what is required.

Effective and ongoing communication with your child's teachers creates a "web of protection." Adding coaches, counselors, custodians, cafeteria workers, front office staff, administrators, other students, and safety officers to your web is important to ensure there is always someone looking out for your child.

Too frequently, parents are disconnected from their child's school and their children are not connected to other adults and students. While most children enjoy elementary school, the stress of middle and high school can become unbearable.

Between the text messages to our high school son and cell phone calls to his school's safety officers and custodians, someone is always looking out for him.

Not every child will be a whiz at everything. If the information is presented to the child in the way in which he or she best learns; if parents discuss what is being studied with their children at home; if children are encouraged to process or apply what they have learned, then all children should do well.

Children are rarely stretched to their potential. Rarely lifted to the highest level of learning and applying what they know, their potential lies far beyond minimum proficiency levels. Mediocrity is so widespread that genius is unimaginable. Yet, the evidence of genius is witnessed daily. The level at which children compete on basketball courts and in ice skating competitions. The seemingly miraculous ways in which children dribble soccer balls and tumble in gymnastics provides glimpses into their extraordinary potential. Remember, Bodily/Kinesthetic Intelligence is only one of the eight intelligences. Nurturing the artistic, mathematical, scientific, environmental, political, spiritual, musical, and poetic genius of children can also be achieved through consistently and continually heightened expectations.

In our household, learning has always come first. Schoolwork comes before play time. Reading comes before television. While our then, twelve-year-old son, did not always get straight A's we began each grading period with that as our goal. Our then, seven-year-old son, required little motivation. He wanted to score 100 percent on every spelling test. He wanted to learn how to sound out new words. Part of his nightly prayers were, "Thank you God for helping me to become the most handsome little boy in the world and thank you God for helping me to become the smartest little boy in the world." His room has always been full of books and he takes pride in being able to pick up and read any book on his bookshelf.

Be aware of times when your child is intensely focused on a particular project, game, or other activity. Notice whether there is a refreshed, joyful, or relaxed expression on your child's face after he has completed the activity. This may also tell you that he has had an important learning experience that has touched his natural genius.

[*Awakening Your Child's Natural Genius*]

Keep your child ahead of the game

Consider introducing your children to subjects and content areas before they are covered in their classrooms. Give them a head start whenever possible. Get them into the habit of completing their assignments before the due date and preparing for tests well in advance. Again, their potential lies far beyond what is being covered at any particular grade level. Our younger son provided a wonderful example of this when he came home from his first-grade class and declared, "Mom, I am going to take my spelling test on Thursday because my teacher allows all of the students who always get 100 percent to take the test early."

An undeniable challenge confronting us as parents is to have high expectations without placing too much pressure on our children. Even while affirming high expectations we need to hug our children more and scold them less, praise their efforts and be less critical of their struggles, and celebrate their wins and accept their losses. There have been times when I have been disappointed in my children's efforts and on more than one occasion I have had to put myself into time-out. There is a thin line between pushing your child and pressuring your child and perhaps an even thinner line between expecting excellence and accepting failure. We push our sons to do well in whatever they do, however, both Nina and I work hard not to pressure them as to make the experience, itself, an unhappy one. Like most parents, we are not always successful. When we know that we have blown it, Nina and I both apologize to our children. (Mom and dad are human too!)

Keep in mind that you should be your child's best coach and most enthusiastic cheerleader. You should help each of your children to tap their divinely-given infinite wells of capacity as they reach for the best within themselves. Admittedly, it may often result in a tug of war; however, allow love to guide you.

- Avoid becoming angry with your child but be a firm coach when needed.

- Teach your child how to be responsible by modeling responsible behavior.

- Never ridicule your child. No matter how tired or frustrated you become, always use positive and encouraging language.

- Push, but do not pressure.

- Work hard on maintaining a constant tone of voice. Being firm does not require yelling, screaming, threatening, or ridiculing.

- Never forget that your child is just that, a child.

- Keep a tally of how many times you point out what you child has done wrong during any given day and compare that to the number of times you praised your child.

- Keep a tally of how many times you hug your child each day and say, "I love you."

More than one parent has heard a child scream or whisper, "I can't stand you" or "I hate you." More than one parent has wanted to say, "I hate you too!" Keep in mind, "this too shall pass."

Teacher Strategies

- Send parents a one page sheet outlining typical developmental behaviors, e.g., "What to Expect from Your Middle School Child."

- Advise parents of your ongoing means of communication, e.g., student agenda, Traffic Light Book, subject-area binder, etc.

- Teach students how to use the communication tool and use it as part of an extra-credit grade.

- Provide timely intervention when communication is failing.

- Provide frequent opportunities for parent intervention in retaking tests/quizzes, making up homework, and completing class projects.

S tep 7

Prepare for School

S tep back and take a look at your household and assess what must be done to prepare for the school year. If organization is not one of your strengths, ask friends, relatives, or other parents to help you get organized and prepared for the first day of school.

The following steps will help you to organize yourself and your household:

1. Get the school district calendar and post the first day of school onto your refrigerator. Your goal is to have everything organized and all of the necessary paperwork completed at least one week prior to the first day of school.

2. Ask the school for a supply list for the forthcoming school year.

   If your child's school does not provide a supply list, this would be a perfect opportunity for you to volunteer.

Three weeks prior to the end of the school year we received a supply list from our son's elementary school listing all of the required supplies, by grade level, for the next school year. The list also indicated which supplies would be sold by the PTA during the Meet and Greet day.

3. Establish the following boxes, drawers, or permanent locations in your home:

    • School box—used to keep all school related papers.

    • Supply box—used for all school supplies.

    • Resource box—used for such resources as Dictionary, Atlas, Thesaurus, grammar guide, math/science study guides, etc.

    • The book, *A High School Plan for Students with College-Bound Dreams*, is a valuable resource for parents of high school students. The book outlines how to prepare boxes for college applications, financial-aid information, and other important papers pertaining to the college admissions process.

4. Request the following information from the school prior to the end of the current school year:

    - Student registration form
    - School calendar
    - Immunization schedule

5. Complete the school's registration form and gather any information required to register your child for the forthcoming school year (e.g., immunization records, birth certificate, social security card, proof of address, etc.). Now is the time to identify your emergency contacts and people who will be authorized to pick up your child from school. Parents of college-bound students will have to gather their tax information and W2 forms to be prepared to complete their FAFSA and other financial-aid information.

6. Get five large envelopes; write your child's name; and the name, address, and telephone number of the school onto each envelope.

7. Place the following information into each envelope (note: some of the information may not be available until after the first day of school):

   - Your contact information (i.e., work phone, cell phone, pager, work hours, lunch time, etc.).

   - A copy of your child's class schedule.

   - The name and contact information of each teacher.

   - The names of the administrators, office staff, and your child's counselor.

   - Locker information, including the location and combination of your child's locker.

   - Bus number, including pick-up and drop-off times.

8. Place one envelope into your car, one at your job, one into your school box, and give one to each of the emergency contacts who you authorize to pick up your child from school.

9. Review the supply lists, purchase the necessary school supplies, and place them into the supply box.

   Typical supplies would include:

   - Three-hole college-ruled paper
   - Spiral notebooks
   - Plain unlined white paper
   - Construction paper
   - Tape
   - Glue sticks
   - Paper clips
   - Staples
   - Colored pencils, markers, or crayons
   - #2 Pencils and ink pens (black and red)
   - Erasers
   - Highlight markers
   - White out
   - Three ring folders/binders
   - Clear report covers

10. Purchase or gather the needed resource materials and place into the resource box.

    Typical resource materials would include:

    - Dictionary
    - Thesaurus

- English Grammar Guide
- Atlas
- Pencil sharpener
- Calculator
- Ruler
- Stapler
- Scissors
- Three-hole puncher

11. Identify a permanent location for backpacks, lunch boxes, and soiled athletic clothes (i.e., P.E. uniform, jerseys, etc.).

12. Establish your school day routine such as:

- Wake-up time
- Bedtime
- Homework time and study location
- Morning and evening routines (e.g., bath, vitamins, reading, laying out clothes, etc.)

13. Post a calendar in your kitchen and write all of the important school dates onto the calendar (i.e., standardized testing, short days, holidays, progress reports, report cards, parent-teacher conferences, PTA/PTSA meetings, spring break, etc.).

Once you establish your routine, try to maintain the same routine every night of the school year. Post the homework rules in the place where your child will do his or her homework.

We have a file cabinet drawer devoted to school-related papers for each of our children. With good intentions we attempted to maintain a separate folder for each subject and special interest area by grading period, however, we soon discovered that it was easier and less stressful to simply dump all of the papers into our school box as they come home. We go through all of the important papers as soon as they come home but there are so many papers our children bring home from school that we just do not have time to go through all of them as soon as they come home. We have learned that as long as we dump everything into the school box we are assured that everything is in one place. At the end of the school year we organize all of our children's schoolwork and develop a scrap book of the school year.

Homework Rules

Whatever you decide upon for your homework rules (see sample on next page), be sure that you do not allow your child an opportunity to do the things that are important to him (e.g., talking on the telephone, television, video games, sports, etc.) until he has completed his schoolwork and whatever else is important to you.

Homework Rules

1. Begin all homework within 30 minutes of getting home from school.

2. Place all homework into a stack on the kitchen table when completed.

3. Homework must be reviewed and error-free before you can leave the table.

4. All error-free assignments are worth 10 minutes of television time (maximum television on school nights is 30 minutes).

5. Read for 30 minutes after homework is completed.

6. No company or telephone calls until after homework and reading has been completed.

7. Clean up your area and put away your books and supplies after completing your homework.

Create a work environment consistent with what you outlined earlier as your child's learning style. While background music is good for one child, it may be distracting for another. If you allow your child to listen to background music while he does his homework, try to make sure that it is music only, no vocals. No matter what your child says, the lyrics are likely to interrupt his concentration. He is more likely to remember the lyrics to the song rather than the words or facts in the book he is reading.

If you have children who differ in their learning styles, try to accommodate each of them. For example one child may work best at a table and chair while another works best lying across a bed, one may work best under dim lighting while the other works best in a brightly lit room.

Develop consistent routines

Post the school calendar in a location where it will remain for the entire school year. In our home the kitchen is the ideal location and the central gathering place for the family each school day. Also, find a location (like a wall or the side of the refrigerator) where you can post all of the test preparation papers (i.e., spelling words, geography facts, grammar, etc.). Use these papers to quiz your children each day during breakfast, dinner, or just before bedtime. Consistently follow the routines you have establish for bedtime, dinner time, etc. Help your child to become accustomed to consistent routines such as brushing his teeth "before" he gets dressed.

If this sounds a bit regimented, it is. There are so many papers that come home, so much work to be done, so many special notes and notices from the school, and so much schoolwork to stay on top of that getting yourself and your family organized at the beginning of the school year can mean the difference between great grades and average grades, between high test scores and low test scores, between a stress-free and stressful school year. A well-organized household helps to reduce everyone's stress level and helps your children to have the best opportunity to succeed. Keep in mind that a child's journey from kindergarten through high school graduation is a thirteen year journey. A child's success each school either provides a foundation to build upon or a hindrance to success at the next grade level. How successful you are at preparing for, and supporting your child, each school year can make the difference between success and failure.

As a first-grader, our son woke up at 6:00 a.m. so that he would be ready to catch the school bus at 7:05 a.m. Our seventh-grader woke up at 7:00 a.m. so that he could catch his bus at 8:40 a.m. Both of our children had regular routines and morning responsibilities. The consistent routines helped everyone to be successful and to get a stress-free start. Their clothes were ironed and laid out the night before. In fact, our seventh-grader was responsible for putting together ten outfits, five each for he and his brother, on Sunday evening.

The evening routine was occasionally difficult as a result of school-related activities—baseball, basketball, track and field, soccer, etc. However, when we got home they both did their homework, ate dinner, showered, put their pajamas on, brushed their teeth, and got ready for bed. They both had such full schedules that there was rarely time for television or video games during the school week. Any extra time was usually spent reading or spending time together as a family. After all of this, they said their prayers. We hugged, kissed, and they were off to bed.

While some people might think that this sounds more like, "Leave it to Beaver" than reality in America, this was our household and these were the regular routines with our sons. The routines changed as our children grew older and entered into new school settings. As they have grown older, matured, and become responsible for developing and maintaining their own routines, my wife and I have structured our lives accordingly. As parents, we are responsible for structuring the environment that our sons need to assist them in going as far as their talents and abilities will take them in school and in life.

The many demands on parents and families, will make it difficult to maintain regular routines. However, do the best that you can and do not make excuses. If you organize yourself early and help your family to work together as a team, there is nothing that you and your family cannot accomplish. Older siblings can quiz younger children. Younger children can talk about what happens at school while they are taking a bath. Children who are good at math can tutor siblings. There are all sorts of talents, gifts, and abilities you can draw upon within your family.

Whenever I travel, my wife, in essence, becomes a single parent. Being organized is the only way that she makes it. She learned the hard way how important it is to be organized.

When our older son was in fourth grade and our younger son was in preschool, I was traveling on average two weeks out of each month. During the first few months of my heavy travel schedule, my wife was, in a word, worn out. Each night that I called from the hotel, she rarely had anything positive to say:

"You know what your son did today? I got a call from the school today about Jalani. I'm going to have to go up to the school tomorrow to find out why Mychal-David's grades have fallen off so much from the last grading period!"

It got to be so bad that I stopped calling home and began sending my wife e-mail messages instead. When I returned home, I tried to sit down with my wife and look at the household routines, but she did not want to do that. She was convinced that it had nothing to do with the routines. It was because I was gone that my sons had lost their minds! Fortunately, my travel slowed down just before the holiday break. Following the holiday break, my wife decided that she was going to leave me, my boys, and my routines to fend for ourselves. She was going to Jamaica with a group of her girlfriends.

The weekend before my wife left, I organized the entire school week. I prepared seven outfits for each of my sons and hung them in their closet. Jalani and Mychal-David could choose their outfit each morning. On Sunday, after church, I prepared dinner for the entire week. I created a listing of individual responsibilities for each day of the week. The consequence was going to bed 15 minutes early for each neglected responsibility. They had two breakfast choices each day that were selected the night before. If they did not give me their choice the night before, it was automatically "Dad's choice."

Needless to say, each day that my wife called, the boys and I told her how well everything was going. She never believed us. When she returned from Jamaica, I gave her a copy of our routine. She adopted most of it and discovered that it worked for her as well.

Following is a list of things that all parents should consider—whether single, teen, grand, foster, or overworked:

- Establish a consistent bedtime and wake-up time for your children.

- Develop a diet of proper nutrition. If children had their way many would live off of hotdogs, breakfast cereal, and candy. As the parent, you are suppose to know better.

  As soon as your children get up, they must have something to eat. If not breakfast, then a piece of fruit.

- Make sure your child does his or her homework. If the work is too difficult for you to help with, tell your child's teacher so that she can help you find a mentor or tutor.

- Make sure that your child takes a shower or bath each night or each morning.

- Make sure your child brushes his or her teeth and flosses. As the saying goes, "Pay me now or pay me later." Teaching a child how to take care of his or her teeth will help him or her learn good habits that will sustain them as an adult. Either take care of your teeth or lose them! Gum disease causes many people to lose their teeth prematurely and unnecessarily.

- Send your child to school clean, with his hair brushed or combed, prepared mentally and physically to learn. If you have a son, make sure that he wears a belt and that his pants are pulled up appropriately.

  If you leave for work before your child leaves for school, ask the teacher to send you a note each day letting you know that your child was clean and that his or her hair was combed.

- Organize your child's clothes and school supplies each night.

  We lay out a full week's of clothes on Sunday and allow our sons to pick their outfits each school day.

- Show an interest in what your child is learning. Talk to your child each day about what is happening in school.

- Continually reinforce that schoolwork and reading comes before watching television, playing video games, or talking on the telephone.

- Prepare a quiet, consistent, and uninterrupted place for studying.

Preparing for school is more than just having *things* organized; it is having *yourself* organized. How successful you are in helping your child to have a great start to the school year can mean the difference between success and failure.

Teacher Strategies

- Provide supply list, opportunities for free or donated supplies, and steps for organizing supplies and a study location at home.

- Provide the course syllabus, sample grading rubric, and "tips for academic success."

- Provide sample "test language" with accompanying vocabulary and definitions.

- Provide "key points" for getting a jump on learning, (e.g, high carb breakfast, recognizing time-of-day energy levels, reviewing important facts and concepts each evening, etc.).

- Advise parents of predictable student behaviors (e.g, boys are less organized than girls, failure to take effective notes, ineffective test preparation, etc.).

S tep 8

Prepare for Testing

Your child's performance on classroom and standardized tests will impact his or her class placement, course offerings, and opportunities to participant in summer camps and enrichment programs. If you have a lot of money your children may not have to do well in school or on standardized tests. If you have enough money you can probably buy their way into a college somewhere. However, if you do not want to be stuck with an enormous college bill or stuck with an unemployed child the rest of your life, do all that you can to help him or her to get good grades and do well on standardized tests.

It was our older son's scores on the Iowa Test of Basic Skills (ITBS) that qualified him for the Talented and Gifted program. The teachers and subjects that he was exposed to in his gifted classes provided him with many expanded learning opportunities.

His grades in fifth grade, together with his test scores in fourth grade, had an impact on his placement in advanced academic classes in middle school.

His success on tests helped to increase his self-esteem and to convince him that he was as smart as anyone else. Also, with each success came greater test-taking confidence that, in turn, helped him to deal with the natural anxiety of preparing for and taking standardized tests.

While good grades can provide your child with a broad range of academic awards and recognition, high test scores can provide your child with a wide range of opportunities from elementary through high school and scholarship money for college. Ultimately, grades and standardized test scores will determine the scope of your child's college choices. Your child's success in school will also have an impact on the range of programs, camps, activities, and clubs that he or she may have the opportunity to participate in.

In many school districts, high test scores will qualify your child for the Talented and Gifted Program; academically-gifted classes; high school honors and AP classes; state, local, and national competitions; academic-oriented clubs (e.g., National Honor Society, Beta Club, etc.); and place your child into classes with some of the school district's highest performing students.

Despite the fact that schools throughout the country are being measured by how well students perform on standardized tests, parents typically receive very little information advising them of what they can do to help their child perform well on such tests. Not only will higher test scores help your child's school meet your State Accountability Standards they will provide your child with opportunities to do more interesting and engaging work. Typically, schools with low test scores devote a significant amount of time preparing students to perform better on state or district-mandated tests. Schools that are already performing well devote more time to engaging students in projects, performances, extracurricular activities, field trips, and more academically-related rather than test-driven learning opportunities.

Doing well on tests

Performing well on tests, as is a child's performance in athletic competitions, requires practice, coaching, focus, and preparation. Anything you can do to support, encourage, and prepare your child do well is in the best interest of your child!

The following steps will help you help your child do better on tests within the classroom:

1. Get advance notice from each of your child's teachers about tests and quizzes.

   Our son's first-grade teacher gave students their spelling words on Monday and tested them on Friday. We posed the spelling words on the refrigerator and reviewed the words with our son each morning at breakfast. By Friday, he had talked about, spelled, and prepared for the spelling test all week. He averaged 100 percent for the entire school year!

   Our son's seventh-grade science teacher provided a monthly calendar of lectures, assignments, and tests at the beginning of each month. We posted the calendar on the refrigerator and discussed the information that our son was learning in class throughout the month and made sure we did not schedule any activities on the nights prior to his tests. This process helped us to help our son maintain an A average in Science, Math, and Language Arts. Being prepared throughout the school year helped to reduce everyone's stress level.

2. Talk about what will be covered on tests at home before and after school each day.

3. Review the material and test your child at home several times before tests are given in class.

4. Find out the way in which your child most easily processes and recalls information.

For example, one child can easily remember facts when they are studied in alphabetical order. For another child, the facts must be memorized as a rap or poem. Another child must put the facts into a song. Another child must write the facts down each night before going to bed. While yet another child must have the facts placed onto an audio tape so that he or she can play back the tape after dinner, during the ride to and from school, or while taking a bath!

5. The night before the test, make sure that your child gets a good night's sleep and has a healthy breakfast on the morning of the test.

Tests vary by state, school district and by level of schooling (i.e., elementary, middle, and high school). Every parent must know the tests that are given, when they are given, and how they will impact class placement, advancement to the next grade, high school graduation, and/or college enrollment.

Standardized test dates vary by school district and by grade level. Some school districts give children different types of tests. In second and fourth grades in Georgia, students take the Iowa Test of Basic Skills (ITBS.) During fifth grade in Florida, students take the Florida Comprehensive Achievement Tests (FCAT), and the Comprehensive Test of Basic Skills (CTBS). Many states require that students pass high school exit exams prior to receiving their high school diplomas.

Ask your child's teacher or counselor if they will be doing practice tests, how you can help your child at home, and if there are study guides available to help your child prepare. Get a copy of the study guides as soon as possible and help your child study from them as often as you can. If your child demonstrates an interest and is capable of studying books beyond his or her grade level, encourage him or her to do so. We are only beginning to understand the complexities of the human brain and its extraordinary potential.

The following steps will help your child prepare for standardized testing:

1. Get a schedule of the standardized test dates. Post the dates on your refrigerator or in a place where you will be sure to notice them.

2. Ask the school for sample tests or for study sheets and study them with your child throughout the school year.

3. Encourage your child each day during the week of testing as he or she leaves home and praise your child's effort each day as he or she returns home.

4. Encourage your child to read and use test language (e.g., compare, contrast, mean, median, sum, etc.).

   Slang and today's hip-hop language will not help your child to perform well on standardized tests. Using language in the way in which your child is likely to read it on tests will.

5. Prepare in advance, your child's clothes for each day of the week of testing.

6. Ensure that your child gets plenty of rest each night before testing.

7. Ensure that your child has a healthy breakfast each morning.

8. Ensure that your household is as quiet and as peaceful as possible during the week of testing.

9. Keep after-school activities to a minimum during the week of testing.

10. Review and practice material each night before testing.

    For example, practice math the night before the Math Test and review social studies facts the evening before the Social Studies Test.

11. Encourage and help your child to relax each morning of testing. Do not pressure him or her to do well, just encourage him or her to do his or her best.

12. Ask your child's teacher for test-taking and test preparation strategies.

13. Reinforce the test-taking strategies each morning with your son or daughter.

    For example, we tell our son each morning to remember to place a check next to those questions he is not sure of. When he has answered all of the questions, he should go back and take another look at each of the questions he has placed a check next to until the time is up.

14. Have a celebration at the end of testing. Have a pizza party, go to a movie, or go to the park. Let your children know you are pleased with their effort.

Following these steps has helped us to help both of our sons do well on standardized tests throughout elementary, middle, and high school. After receiving your child's test scores, go over them with your child's teacher or counselor to identify weak areas. Ask if the scores qualifies your child for advanced classes or for the Talented and Gifted program. If not, how far from qualifying is he or she? Get a head start helping your child strengthen any weak areas. Remember more testing will come next year. Keep a copy of each year's test scores in your school box.

High test scores do not mean that your child is any smarter than low test scores indicate that he or she is not very smart. Some students are better at taking tests than others. Some students have had a good match of their learning styles with their teachers' teaching styles. Some students remember facts and concepts easily while others find it more difficult. No matter how well or how poorly your child does, always remind him or her that he or she is a divine creation, a continuing work in progress.

Not only do all children have the potential for creative accomplishment, but all children should have goals that will challenge them and a vision that will lead them to be the best they can be. Is this view naive or idealistic, especially when we consider teens who don't know how to read or write? Edison was thrown out of public school and described as mentally addled and unteachable. Einstein had difficulties in school, especially with math. We should be cautious about predicting a limited future for any child. Instead, we should always leave room for youngsters to work toward challenges that are beyond "just getting by."

[Bringing Out The Giftedness In Your Child]

While you may not be able to choose your child's friends, you can influence his or her peers through the programs and activities which you enroll, or encourage your child to participate in.

Beware of peer pressure

As a final note, be conscious of peer pressure. Many schools still struggle to foster a culture of high academic achievement. Schools have huge trophy cases to celebrate their athletic teams with athletes receiving letters, sweaters, jackets, and special consideration throughout the school and community. No letters, sweaters, jackets, fanfare, or celebration are directed toward the academic scholars. Football trophies may stand three feet or taller, while the National Merit Scholars, National Essay winner, Science Fair winner, etc., have small plaques, certificates, or name plates (2 x 1 inch) to recognize their extraordinary academic achievement. Banners hang in front of and around the school celebrating the City Basketball and State Football championships. There are no banners celebrating the State Science Fair winner or the National Spelling Bee winner. Athletes receive huge letters while the honor students receive small ribbons. All of these send signals to students that academic achievement is not as highly valued or as noticeably celebrated as athletic achievement. Athletes have a highly publicized National Signing Day while scholars simply graduate and quietly go off to enroll into some of the country's top academic institutions. Peer pressure not to do well in school begins in elementary school and is in full force in high schools where students attend school each day with the single-minded purpose of socializing and playing sports. Children who get high grades and high test scores are rarely celebrated and more frequently picked on or called names.

Help your child to overcome the inevitable negative peer pressure by developing your vision early and by celebrating academic achievement in your household, church, and throughout your family and community. It also helps if you can provide opportunities for your children to excel in areas beyond academics. Sports, cheer leading, martial arts, music, dance, band, photography, skating, and student government, all help to expand your child's horizons and broaden his or her circle of friends. Our older son has played 3 varsity sports in high school (football, lacrosse, and track and field) while taking a rigorous academic schedule. We must continually encourage and support young people in their pursuit of a broad range of academic and extracurricular activities.

Children Learn What They Live

If children live with criticism, they learn to condemn.

If children live with hostility, they learn to fight.

If children live with ridicule, they learn to be shy.

If children live with shame, they learn to feel guilty.

If children live with encouragement, they learn confidence.

If children live with tolerance, they learn patience.

If children live with praise, they learn to appreciate.

If children live with acceptance, they learn to love.

If children live with approval, they learn to like themselves.

If children live with honesty, they learn truthfulness.

If children live with security, they learn to have faith in themselves and others.

If children live with friendliness, they learn the world is a nice place in which to live.

— Dorothy Law Nolte

S tep 9

Talk About
What Your Child is Learning

Demonstrate an interest in what your child is working on in school. Get into the habit of saying to your child each day after school, "Tell me what happened in school today." Show enthusiasm about the things your child is excited about and try to find ways of getting your child to be excited about things that have to be learned but may not be interesting.

Our older son studied archeology in third grade. We took copies of his archeology facts with us during spring break and talked about archeology in the car during our drive from Atlanta, Georgia, to Washington, D.C. When studying state capitals in fourth grade, we quizzed him each day at the grocery store, in the barber shop, and at the mall. He liked it so much that he began asking adults if they knew certain state capitals. "Mr. Ralston, I'll bet you don't know the state capital of Maine. Ms. Kimberly, I'll bet you don't know the state capital of Alaska."

Look around your home for things related to subjects your child is studying in school: weights and measures in the kitchen and at the gas station; temperature readings on your thermostat, or the temperature of water boiling on the stove versus water used to take a shower; the cost of food at the grocery store; the wattage of light bulbs; the chemical makeup of the detergents used for laundry.

Reading is everything. Talk to your child about the books that he or she is reading in school. Have your child read to you. Your son can read to you while you prepare dinner. Your daughter can read to you during the drive to and from school. Encourage older children to share their stories with younger siblings.

Every child should be encouraged to read at least one book per week from the time they learn to read until they graduate high school. Our then, seven-year-old son Jalani, read on average, 3 books each evening after school. Now, as a twelve-year-old, he is consistently at the top of his middle school class. Yet, we, like many parents, undergo a constant tug-of-war as he would rather play video games than read. Needless to say, he would rather spend time at the video game store than at the bookstore. Our responsibility as parents is to ensure that he spends time in the bookstore, he can find his own way to the video game store.

Parents should provide children with as many books as they do toys, basketball shoes, CDs, video games, and designer clothes if they are to see noticeable improvements in their children's achievement levels and success in school. Reading is one of the most important keys to success in life. Reading is not an option it is a necessity; television, radio, and music videos are options.

> *When our older son was in the first grade he had a class assignment to count things at home (e.g., the number of cereal boxes, beds, chairs, etc.). One of the items on his list required that he count all of the books in his room. Nina and I were pleasantly surprised that our son counted 320 books! All of those books were passed on to his younger brother, who, as a first grader, had over 500 books.*

While working with fourth- and fifth-grade students at Bond Elementary School in Tallahassee, Florida, in several classrooms I asked students to set a personal goal of how many books they could read in three days? Once each student affirmed the number of books he or she would personally commit to reading I tallied all of the books to arrive at a class total. One classroom affirmed they could read 77 books within the three day period. That Friday, I visited their classroom and was pleasantly surprised to hear that not only had they reached their goal of 77 books but they had actually read 132 books! Setting goals leads to high achievement and high goals evolve from having high expectations.

High Expectations

Help your child to strengthen his or her academic abilities by spending more time studying in his or her weakest subjects. How much work your child does should not be a function of how much work the teacher assigns. You must help your child understand what his or her weaknesses are. It is analogous to working out on weights; when you know your legs or abdominal muscles are weak you have to work harder to strengthen them. Although you are likely to feel better about yourself when you look in the mirror and flex those muscles which are most highly developed (e.g., chest, shoulders, biceps, and triceps), you have to consciously work on the muscle groups that are least developed (e.g., legs and abdominal muscles). Learning, like bodybuilding or any sport, requires that you practice, practice, practice. The more you practice, the better you become. Each person will be strong in some areas and weak in others.

Many children, like many athletes, would prefer to spend their time working in the areas where they are already strong. They, like most people, feel better about the things they can do well. However, our responsibility as parents is to help our children strengthen their weaknesses. All children will struggle with something—matn, science, reading, writing, time management, organization, note taking, or social skills. Boys, particularly, struggle with organizing themselves for the elementary to middle school transition. Do not excuse your child's weaknesses, "Well he is not a good writer. I wasn't a good writer." Whether it is his math performance or turning in his homework, he will need you to have high expectations and to provide the necessary patience and support so he is able to meet those expectations.

To help your child master subjects in school you do not have to go back to school. You only have to develop a plan. Keep the facts that he is studying with you; at home; in the car; or at your desk at work. Take advantage of every opportunity to talk about his schoolwork. The more you talk about his schoolwork, the more seriously he will take his schoolwork. If you are interested, he will become interested. Develop a series of rewards for extra work. We do not believe in rewarding our children for what is expected, i.e., doing their homework and completing their class work. However, if our son can recite all fifty state capitals a week before the test, we will treat him to something special. If he can recall facts relating to his forthcoming social studies, math, language arts, or vocabulary test a week before the test, we may celebrate with some extra television time. We used to give our then, seven-year-old son, verbal math problems while riding in the car: "What is two plus three, times five, plus five, times three, plus ten, plus ninety-nine, plus one, divided by two?" If he got the right answer of one hundred, we would buy him some ice cream. Now, as a seventeen-year-old high school student, we get daily text messages:

"95 on test in Political Science."

"81 on AP Psychology test."

"93 on lit paper."

"97 on Chemistry quiz."

One day our older son asked, "Dad do you and mom know how to talk about something other than school?" I responded, "Yes, as soon as you graduate from college."

S tep 10

Stay Focused on the Dream

M ost of us were taught that we should go to school and get a good education so we could get a good job. Now, as adults, many of us are asking, "What was the good education that I was supposed to get?" and, "Where is the good job that it was supposed to guarantee?"

There is not a single type of education that every child needs, however, each child needs to have an education that will enable him or her to pursue his or her dreams and aspirations. Despite all of the things they are taught in the classroom, all of the homework they are given, all of the field trips, all of the research papers, all of the tests, and all of the other stuff they are suppose to remember and are required to know, most children will go to school from kindergarten through the twelfth grade and never have an assignment, homework, or research paper designed to help them discover their *dreams* and *aspirations*.

For over nineteen years, I have worked with thousands of teachers in hundreds of schools throughout the United States and I can tell you, without hesitation, that in American public education, we do not teach dreams. Despite Dr. Martin Luther King, Jr.'s speech, *I Have A Dream*, and despite the many posters and television commercials that talk about, *The Pursuit of the American Dream*, we do not teach children how to discover their dreams and we do not inspire children to pursue their dreams.

Think about it. When you were in school, how many of your teachers, from kindergarten through the twelfth grade, spent any time during the school year talking about your dreams? How many teachers made an attempt to connect what you were learning with what you may have wanted to achieve in life? How many teachers posted student's dreams around the classroom or encouraged or inspired you to do a research paper on what you wanted to achieve in life? How many field trips did you go on that specifically related to your long-term dreams and aspirations? How many guest speakers were invited into your school or classroom who had lived your dreams and who were invited to talk to you about what you must do to achieve your dreams?

While our older son has attended, arguably, the best public schools, from traditional public schools to magnet schools specializing in the arts, he has only, on the rarest occasions, had a classroom activity, lesson or field trip that was specifically designed to help students discover their dreams, define their dreams, learn about their dreams, or pursue their dreams. On the rarest of occasions when he has had such an activity, he has never had any follow up to such an activity or discussion. We just do not teach dreams. We do not talk to children about their dreams and we do not inspire children to dream. This, despite the fact that children are eager learners when it relates to something they are interested in. When our son, Mychal-David, was in the fourth grade, his class took a field trip to the High Museum of Art in Atlanta, Georgia. Following the trip, we received a note from his teacher:

> *"Mychal-David was wonderful. He accompanied the curator and pointed out the various artistic techniques of the artists (abstract, cubism, realism, etc.) and mediums (oils, clay, water colors, pencil, pen and ink, etc.). He pointed out that Pablo Picasso was born in Spain (I thought he was born in France!), and he was the most polite and well-mannered of all of the students."*

Unlike many of the other children, Mychal-David had a *dream* of becoming an artist. This field trip tapped into his *interests* and had a direct connection to his *dreams*. For the other children, it was an opportunity to get away from school and to ride the school bus. This is not to diminish the academic and cultural value of the field trip itself, only to highlight the importance of providing opportunities for more field trips to relate to the wide range of student dreams and aspirations.

As parents and teachers we will never question whether the importance of teaching reading, writing, math, science, social studies, or physical education. Whether children are interested or not, we are going to teach them to read, write, and think. However, in the process of reading, writing, and thinking our children are more likely to be encouraged to write a letter to the Easter Bunny than to someone who is living his or her dream. He or she is more likely to write five papers on Christopher Columbus than one paper on his or her dreams. He or she is more likely to be taught math in the abstract rather than in a meaningful way for applying math to fulfilling his or her dreams. He or she will likely research and write papers on any number of topics which he or she is uninterested in, and is unlikely to ever refer to as an adult, than he or she is to be directed toward one research paper or writing activity relating to his or her passions, personal interests, or long-term dreams and aspirations.

I suggested to one of my son's teachers that she allow time for her students to discuss their dreams and aspirations. I even offered to come in and lead the students through a discussion, following which, they could write about their dreams or make collages with words and photos pertaining to their dreams. After all, it was nearing the end of the school year and the students had never had an opportunity to discuss the types of things they wanted to achieve in life. They had never talked about how they would use what they had learned during the school year to pursue their dreams and aspirations. In fact, few of the students knew what types of things their classmates wanted to achieve.

My son's teacher politely said, "Thank you for your offer but we do not have time to talk about that. Our schedule is packed through the end of the school year." Between that time and the end of the school year, I asked my son if there was ever any free time in his class. I discovered that almost everyday, the children had free time, much of which was undirected during which they generally just clowned around, yet, his teacher could find no time to talk about students' dreams?

To ensure that your child gets the most out of school and gets the best education, help your child to discover his or her dreams early and take advantage of the many opportunities through his classes, before- and after-school programs, summer camps, and community programs to nurture his or her dreams.

When our older son, Mychal-David, was in the second grade, we were receiving a call from his school at least twice a week, sometimes twice a day, regarding his behavior. Eventually, we were called in to have a conference with his teacher and the school's counselor. They wanted to know, "Is there anything wrong with Mychal?" His teacher commented, "Mychal-David does not want to do his class work and often does not pay attention in class. He sits at his desk doodling when he should be working on his schoolwork."

When my wife and I sat him down to give him a good talking to about his behavior and about not paying attention in class, we could see that he was more motivated to draw than he was to do math and science. He also was not interested in backing down from a fight and was getting into trouble because other children would talk about him or pick on him and he would just go at it.

My wife and I helped our son to place his interest in drawing into the context of a dream—becoming an artist. We enrolled him in after-school art classes, we made art the theme of our household for Christmas, and we enrolled him in a summer art camp.

To help with his behavior, we enrolled him into martial arts. We refocused his aggression on developing a dream of receiving a black belt.

Over time, his behavior changed. He read more books and became interested in re-illustrating the stories. He began putting energy into his art work after school and focusing more on his schoolwork during class. He learned new painting and drawing techniques. The focusing and concentration skills being developed in art class, and in his martial arts training, carried over into math. His martial arts training also further reinforced the at-home lessons we were teaching pertaining to self-control and respect for others. He learned how to control his temper and how to be a good student. His grades and test scores soared and he began to like school more. Each success, experienced through achieving the small dreams—a week without a behavioral problem, a 100 percent score on a spelling test, a story read and illustrated, breaking a board in karate— all helped to inspire our son to develop bigger and greater dreams and to set short- and long-term goals.

Our younger son, Jalani, has always been fascinated with cars. Whenever we were driving along he would call out the names of the various automobiles we passed. His fascination with cars evolved into a dream of owning a Porche dealership and becoming a professional race car driver. As if that was not grand enough, he expanded his dream to owning two dealerships; a Porche and a Jaguar dealership.

Dreams are more than jobs

When we talk about dreams, we too frequently think of jobs. Yes, there are in fact "dream jobs," but jobs are often vehicles that carry us to other dreams, e.g., paying for our child's education, taking a cruise, feeding the hungry, reducing crime, publishing a book, starting a business, buying a home, buying a new car, etc. Help your child to develop short-term dreams and long-term dreams, each leading to short-term goals and long-term goals. Consider the following:

- What types of things does your child enjoy doing?

  For example, does he or she like playing video games, going to the movies, going to a theme park, riding a bicycle, going to a baseball game, drawing, talking, singing, playing an instrument, acting, dressing up, cooking, shopping, etc.? Use his or her interests to inspire dreams of doing, of seeing, of overcoming, of learning, or of changing.

- What talents, special abilities, or intelligences does your child have that could lead to his or her dream career?

  The child who talks a lot could dream of becoming a motivational speaker or television personality. The child who likes to draw could dream of becoming a cartoonist or computer animator. The child who enjoys cooking could dream of becoming a chef or of owning a restaurant. The possibilities are endless!

- What subjects in school does your child enjoy most?

  The child who loves history could dream of becoming an Historian. The child who loves math could dream of becoming an astronaut or mathematician. The child who loves English or literature could dream of becoming a writer, publisher, playwright, or English teacher. The child who loves science could dream of becoming a doctor or research scientist. The child who loves sports could dream of becoming an athlete, sports commentator, orthopedic surgeon, personal fitness trainer, coach, or health club owner.

- Look at each area of your child's seemingly negative behaviors (talking too much, tapping on his or her desk, clowning around in class) and think of positive uses to inspire long-term dreams and aspirations.

Perhaps one of the greatest challenges we have as parents is that we are limited in our own imaginations. Our vision of the child who draws is one of a struggling artist. Whereas, the aspiring artist can pursue graphic arts, computer animation, advertising, web page design, logos, book illustrations, silkscreening, sign making, magazines, newspapers, brochures, political campaigns, interior design or countless other opportunities. Our vision of the aspiring musician is one a struggling nightclub musician. With a little imagination, we could see the possibilities of creating musical scores, commercial jingles, video game or television show themes, elementary school lyrics, or even nap time music. We think of the aspiring professional athlete only in terms of the unlikelihood of his or her achieving such a goal. With a little imagination, we could see the possibilities of becoming a sports agent, team owner, clothing manufacturer, marketing consultant, or automobile dealer (for all of the millionaire athletes who love to spend their money on expensive cars). Open your imagination and open your child to the endless possibilities, to the excitement of pursuing a dream.

Thanks to my mother and, later, Mr. Washington, I grew up with the subconscious conviction that I was going to be somebody, and because of that, there was not going to be room in my life for drugs, alcohol or criminal behavior. Many of those I grew up with foresaw no purpose in their lives. For them, there was no strength of conviction to empower them to resist the allure of drugs and alcohol and crime.

[Les Brown, Live Your Dreams]

You can help to expand your children's imaginations (and yours too) by buying books, videos, audio tapes, or computer software that immerses them into their dreams. Teach your children how to research their dreams in the library and on the Internet. Subscribe to magazines and fill your home with books about the many things your child is interested in. From athletics to architecture, culinary arts to oceanography, modeling to model building, rapping to furniture restoration, automotive mechanics to aeronautics, hair styling to highway planning, whatever their dream, it has been written about in a book, published in a magazine, or is readily available on the Internet. Create dream posters, collages, and portfolios. Develop a portfolio of papers, research, news articles, and photographs relating to their dreams and aspirations. Fill their rooms with "How To" books. The child who dreams of owning his or her own home is ready to read, "How to Make a Fortune in Real Estate" as soon as he or she affirms their dream. It does not matter how old a child is. It does not matter whether or not he or she has saved a down payment. All that matters is that he or she has expressed an interest. Our job is to nurture, water, fertilize, and allow the sun to shine on the seeds of our children's dreams.

Share your children's dream collages or portfolios with their teachers at the beginning of the school year. This visual can be so inspiring that some teachers will be inspired to set aside time to talk about students' dreams and aspirations. Using your child's dream collage as an example, some teachers will encourage the entire classroom to create dream collages. Just think of it. You and your child can inspire the dreams and aspirations of an entire classroom, maybe even an entire school! Those dreams and aspirations can inspire a culture of academic achievement in your child's school, and your child will have other children to share their dreams and aspirations with.

Reading this book may lead you to believe that my wife and I are perfect parents. Nothing could be further from the truth! We have struggled and stumbled. We have had plans blow up in our faces. We have been called crazy by both friends and family. We have been at odds with teachers and counselors. And, we have routinely dealt with insanity and foolishness from our children.

We have screamed, prayed, and questioned. We have doubted our decisions and questioned our own intelligence at having made such seemingly, "dumb" decisons. We have learned that there are no perfect plans, only prayer and patience.

E pilogue

Things to do at the End of the School Year

After surviving another school year, it is time for a celebration. Spend time with your child at the park, walking on the beach, taking in a movie or going anywhere you and your child feel comfortable and happy. Take time to exhale and to reflect on you and your child's successes through the school year. Rarely does a child qualify for the honor roll without his or her parents putting in a lot of time helping him or her to stay on top of his or her academic tasks. Rarely does a top athlete achieve success without a parent paying registration fees, buying equipment, and taking him or her to practices and tournaments. Rarely does a student win a Spelling Bee of Science Fair without a parent's willingness to turn their home into a training camp or laboratory!

Do some end-of-year processing with your child. As you reflect on the school year consider the following questions for you and your child:

1. How did you feel about each of your teachers?

   - *Take a sheet of paper and write one paragraph describing each teacher.*

   - *Write down five adjectives which best describe each teacher, e.g., caring, positive, boring, engaging, enlightening, fun, nasty, loving, kind, inspiring, encouraging, etc.*

2. What was the most interesting thing you learned in each class or subject?

3. What were the top five things you enjoyed most in school?

4. What were the five worst things you experienced in school?

5. What subjects did you "feel" the smartest in?

6. What subjects did you struggle the most with?

7. What would you have liked the opportunity to have done more of?

8. What would you have liked to have done less of?

9. What did you learn or experience this year that will best prepare you to be successful in school next year?

10. Is there anything that you would like to do or learn over the summer to better prepare you for the next school year?

Use the answers to these questions to help your child write a letter to each teacher sharing your child's likes and dislikes, best and worst learning experiences, and high and low points of the school year. Through this discussion, I have found my children to have very different impressions of the school and its teachers than I did.

I have discovered, on more than one occasion, my son loved teachers whom I did not particularly care for. It is these teachers for whom I have found the letters most valuable. Rather than leaving them with the negative impression they often received from me through my many notes (and possibly my attitude during parent-teacher conferences), they are left with a positive letter from a child who liked them and enjoyed being in their class. Keep a copy of the letters in your school box and send a copy of the letters to the principal.

The answers to your questions, together with your child's letters, provide a glimpse into your child's feelings about the school year. Despite the fact that school districts throughout the country spend billions of dollars testing, grading, and evaluating our children, rarely do they "talk to" or "listen to" our children. It is important for you as a parent to take the time to "talk to" and "listen to" your child. Let your child know that someone cares about what he or she thought about the teachers, the subjects they studied, the field trips they took, and the many things that happened in their lives during the school year. It is important to know the best and worst things that stand out in your child's mind after the school year is over. This will help you to begin planning for the next school year.

Gather all of the your child's work, awards, and special memories from the school year and compile them into a collage, poster, or scrapbook. Share this with your child's teacher at the beginning of the next school year.

Store the rest of your child's school year materials. This year has represented another step toward your child's pursuing his or her dreams and aspirations. Make note of the people (e.g., teachers, coaches, principals, preachers, friends, family, school staff, tutors, etc.) who have played a role in the growth, development, maturation, and nurturing of your child. Take time to update them on your child's progress over the ensuing years as a means of continually thanking them for their role in your child's development and in making them a permanent part of your child's ongoing success.

Our older son is about to graduate from high school and we are sending a newsletter to each of the people, whom over the years have played a role in his growth and development. Through the newsletter we are recognizing their role in the village, (i.e., It takes a village to raise a child). We are sharing his high school accomplishments and some facts about the college he will be enrolling in. Each person, in his or her own way has contributed to his high school success and his forthcoming admission into college.

Finally, keep in mind that the world is changing with each new day. What was considered impossible yesterday is possible today. What was considered unbelievable yesterday is not only believable but commonplace today. Do not measure your child's potential in terms of what you, or he or she, have done or have not done. Encourage your child to dream great dreams and to aspire to do great things. Never forget, "Your child is a continuing work in progress, a lump of coal which you must untiringly polish into a diamond to reveal his or her divine brilliance."

Things to Say to Your Children to Help Them Discover Their Dreams and Aspirations

wow, you are so good at that • you really have a special gift for that • that is outstanding, would you like to learn more about that? • that is remarkable, I bet few people would have done it that way • you like that so much, maybe we could see if there are any special schools or camps where you could learn more about that • you are on your way to becoming a great ... • let's go to the library and see how much we can find out about that • there is a story about someone who is doing what you want to do. Let's write a letter and ask how they got started • I picked up something special for you today that would help you to become a ... • let's see if there are any books or magazines about that • let's ask your teacher if she can help you learn more about doing that • let's create a portfolio so that we can save your work • hi, this is my son, he is going to become a great ... • hi, this is my daughter, she has an extraordinary talent for ... • let's go and see a movie about that • let's see how many books we can find about that • let's create a special place where we can display your work • that is extraordinary, I am so proud of you*

References

Armstrong, Thomas. (1991). *Awakening Your Child's Natural Genius: Enhancing Curiosity, Creativity, and Learning Ability*. Los Angeles, CA: Jeremy P. Tarcher.

Armstrong, Thomas. (1987). *In Their Own Way: Discovering and Encouraging Your Child's Personal Learning Style*. Los Angeles, CA: Jeremy P. Tarcher.

Collins, Marva. (1992). *"Ordinary" Children, Extraordinary Teachers*. Norfolk, VA: Hampton Roads Publishing.

Dunn, R., Dunn, K., and Treffinger, D. (1992). *Bringing Out The Giftedness in Your Child*. New York, NY: John Wiley & Sons.

Gardner, Howard. (1983). *Frames of Mind: The Theory of Multiple Intelligences*. New York, NY: Harper and Row.

Gardner, Howard. (1991). *The Unschooled Mind: How Children Think and How Schools Should Teach*. New York: BasicBooks.

Holt, John. (1964). *How Children Fail*. New York, NY: Dell Publishing.

Holt, John. (1967). *How Children Learn*. New York, NY: Addison-Wesley Publishing.

Keirsey, David and Bates, Marilyn. (1978). *Please Understand Me: Character & Temperament Types*. Del Mar, CA: Prometheus Nemesis Books.

Lazear, David. (1991). *Seven Ways of Knowing: Teaching for Multiple Intelligences.* Palatine, IL: Skylight Publishing.

Myers, Isabel Briggs and Myers, Peter. (1990). *Gifts Differing: Understanding Personality Type.* Palo Alto, CA: CPP Books.

Smutny, J.F., Veenker, Kathleen and Stephen. (1989). *Your Gifted Child: How to Recognize and Develop the Special Talents in Your Child from Birth to Age Seven.* New York, NY: Facts On File.

Wynn, Mychal. (2005). *A High School Plan for Students with College-Bound Dreams.* Marietta, GA: Rising Sun Publishing.

Wynn, Mychal. (2005). *A Middle School Plan for Students with College-Bound Dreams.* Marietta, GA: Rising Sun Publishing.

Wynn, Mychal. (2005). *Empowering African-American Males: Teaching, Parenting, and Mentoring Successful Black Males.* Marietta, GA: Rising Sun Publishing.

Appendix

Mychal-David

Personal Information:

Mychal-David prefers to be called "Mychal-David." He attended a private preschool in Marietta, Georgia, for pre-K and Kindergarten. He attended Mt. Bethel Elementary school for grades 1 through 4. He transferred to a public magnet school of the arts in fifth grade in St. Petersburg, Florida, so that he could further develop his artistic talents, and returned to complete eighth grade at Dickerson Middle School in Marietta, Georgia.

Mychal-David, while often being unmotivated toward academic tasks, has (as the result of being pushed at home) had consistently high grades and standardized test scores. His major difficulties in school are in the areas of organization and time management.

Mychal-David has participated in a variety of summer camps; Space Camp; Christian camp; soccer; art; swimming; etc. Mychal-David has received numerous academic awards; art awards and recognition; and has a black belt in karate.

Mychal-David has lived in Los Angeles, California, Marietta, Georgia, and St. Petersburg, Florida.

Jalani

Personal Information:

Jalani attended a private preschool in Marietta, Georgia. He attended a pre-K program at a Christian preschool in St. Petersburg, Florida. He attended kindergarten and first grade at a public magnet school of the arts in St. Petersburg, Florida, and returned to Marietta, Georgia, to attend Mt. Bethel Elementary School.

Jalani is highly verbal and has picked up the alphabet, reading, and phonics without much difficulty. He is extremely competitive and always eager to participate in group activities.

Jalani plays soccer, basketball, baseball, and swims very well.

Jalani has a passion for cars. Particularly Porches and Jaguars. His current dream is to own an automobile dealership.

Jalani also likes the theme music to movies and books on tape.

Jalani has lived in Marietta, Georgia, and St. Petersburg, Florida.

Mychal-David

Successful Learning Situations:

- Mychal-David benefits from written instructions; clearly defined time lines; and clearly stated rewards and consequences.

- If the work is highly challenging he works well independently. If he is uninterested in the task he is subject to perform poorly.

- Works best in a classroom with an open exchange of ideas and opinions free of negative language and put downs.

- Daily parent communication is important to helping him stay focused.

- Advance notice to parents of tests and quizzes helps to ensure that he is well prepared.

Unsuccessful Learning Situations:

- Open ended assignments requiring self direction with little teacher interaction.

- Classrooms where students clown around or engage in verbal put downs.

- Classrooms with inconsistent discipline policies.

- Working in large groups with lots of talking and socializing.

Jalani

Successful Learning Situations:

- Jalani benefits from clear verbal instructions.
- Jalani is very sociable and benefits from relationships that are established in small groups.
- Needs clearly defined responsibilities, rules and consequences.
- Benefits from daily parent-teacher contact to reinforce his making good personal decisions within the classroom.
- Learns best in classrooms that allow him to talk and move around frequently.
- Works best in a classroom free of negative language and put downs.

Unsuccessful Learning Situations:

- Classrooms with inconsistent discipline policies and frequent verbal put downs.
- Classrooms that have inconsistent routines.
- Classrooms that do not have clearly-defined daily tasks.
- Classroom lacking positive teacher-student and student-student relationships.

Mychal-David

Personality Types: INFP
(Introvert-Intuitive-Feeling-Perceiving)

- Although popular with peers, Mychal-David is highly introverted. *After entering the seventh grade he became highly sociable at school but continues to have a small circle of friends outside of school and appears most comfortable in small group settings.*

- Highly intuitive and likes working on new and challenging problems.

- A "feeling" person who does not deal well with conflicts. Very sensitive to put downs, criticism, and personal conflicts.

- Highly perceptive; has difficulty completing assignments. Organization and time management present ongoing problems.

INFP types excel in fields that deal with possibilities for people, such as counseling, teaching, literature, art, science, and psychology. They work twice as well at tasks they believe in. They are greatly influenced by feelings. They are perfectionists and happiest when working alone. They often prefer the written word as the way to communicate what they feel.

Jalani

Personality Types: ESTP
(Extravert-Sensing-Thinking-Perceiving)

- Highly extraverted; Jalani is constantly talking, singing, asking questions, or expressing ideas and opinions. Easily meets and greets people, makes new friends, and assumes leadership roles.

- Highly sensitive and likes consistency. Prefers routines and knowing what is expected.

- A "thinking" personality who often creates conflicts when things do not go his way. Can be bossy and is highly opinionated.

- Highly judgmental; likes to complete tasks, and does not like interruptions. Comfortable working on tasks for long periods of time.

ESTP types are adaptable, easy-going, and at ease with people. They rely greatly on memory and may struggle with concepts. Able to absorb an immense number of facts, like them, and remember them. They tend to prefer action to conversation. When they sit around they do so in a state of readiness to jump into action.

Mychal-David

Multiple Intelligences:

- Mychal-David is highly visual. He has highly developed freehand drawing skills, works well with computer graphics, and is a highly visual learner.

- Has demonstrated good Verbal Intelligence in the form of articulating his thoughts, ideas, and opinions. Has difficulty organizing his thoughts for written assignments. Performs best when someone asks questions that prompt thoughts, or when using a tape recorder to talk about his ideas prior to writing.

- Has demonstrated good Logical/Mathematical Intelligence. Consistently scores above the 98th percentile on standardized tests. Does well in math and science.

- Has demonstrated an interest in developing his Naturalist Intelligence. He likes to examine rocks, identify cloud formations, weather patterns, and closely examine insects and animals.

- His greatest challenge is in the area of Interpersonal Intelligence. In his desire to make friends and to fit in he is susceptible to peer pressure.

Jalani

Multiple Intelligences:

- Jalani is full of energy and has highly developed Bodily/Kinesthetic Intelligence. He works well with his hands, easily operates computers and video games, and is good at all sports.

- Demonstrates highly developed Verbal/Linguistic Intelligence. Loves to read and easily remembers words spoken in movies and song lyrics. Easily and frequently answers questions, and communicates thoughts, ideas, and opinions.

- Highly developed Interpersonal Intelligence. Gets along well with others and performs well in team sports or group activities.

- Demonstrates an interest in developing Musical/Rhythmic Intelligence. Enjoys singing and dancing. Easily remembers song lyrics, melodies, and the musical scores of movies.

- Demonstrates an interest in further developing Logical/Mathematical Intelligence. Enjoys problem-solving, i.e., figuring out video games, operating the tv/vcr, and figuring out how things work.

Mychal-David

Learning Style:

- Mychal-David's learning style is highly Analytic and responds best to information that is presented step-by-step or fact-by-fact.

- He performs best when working alone or in groups where students talk after they finish working.

- He prefers to read a story rather than having a story read to him.

- He learns best by watching and by receiving written instructions, including lists and summaries.

- He prefers snacking after completing his work.

- He prefers sitting at a table, desk, or chair.

- He works best when he has clearly defined goals and understands what is expected.

- He prefers to learn the facts and how they are connected to the entire concept.

Jalani

Learning Style:

- Jalani's learning style is highly Global. He becomes bored with facts and is more interested in a story relating to the facts to be learned.

- He prefers to work in groups where students talk while they work.

- He prefers to talk while he eats.

- He prefers informal and relaxing seating while he learns.

- He is highly auditory and remembers most of what is said.

- He easily remembers the words to songs and movies.

- He is highly verbal and learns best when he can talk about what is learned.

- He has a good memory and can easily recall what has been discussed.

- He prefers the teacher to read a story. However, if he has heard the story before he will retell the story as the teacher is telling the story!

Index

If you would like arrange for Mr. Wynn to speak to your teacher, parent, or student group contact:

Rising Sun Publishing/Training and Staff Development

(800) 524-2813
E-mail: speaking@rspublishing.com
web page: http://www.rspublishing.com

To purchase additional copies of this or any of our other books visit your local bookstore, our web site, or write:

Rising Sun Publishing
P.O. Box 70906
Marietta, GA 30007-0907

– Other books from Rising Sun Publishing –

A High School Plan for Students with College-Bound Dreams
US Version • [ISBN 1-880463-66-0] • $19.95
Bermudian Version • [ISBN 1-880463-59-8] • $29.95

Easy-to-follow planning guide for high school students. Helps students to understand how grades, standardized tests, behavior, activities, classes, community service, essays, and the billions of available scholarship moneys can all be factored into a plan (beginning in the sixth grade!) that can pave the way into the college(s) of their choice. Provides worksheets for tracking grades, test scores, awards, and class schedules.

A Middle School Plan for Students with College-Bound Dreams
US Version • [ISBN 1-880463-67-9] • $15.95
Bermudian Version • [ISBN 1-880463-70-9] • $19.95

Easy-to-follow planning guide for middle school students. Outlines how to maximize the middle school experience and how to prepare students for high school success as a stepping-stone to students' college-bound dreams. Provides worksheets for tracking grades, test scores, awards, and class schedules.

Don't Quit [ISBN 1-880463-26-1] • $9.95

Mychal Wynn's critically-acclaimed book of poetry contains 26 poems of inspiration and affirmation. Each verse is complemented by an inspiring quotation.

Empowering African-American Males: Teaching, Parenting, & Mentoring Successful Black Males [Wynn]
Book • [ISBN 1-880463-69-5] • $24.95
Workbook • [ISBN 1-880463-71-7] • $15.95

Black males are the most "at-risk" students in America's schools. They are the most likely to be placed into special education, drop out of school, be suspended, be the victims or perpetrators of violent crimes, or be incarcerated. This book outlines a clear, cohesive set of strategies to turn the tide of underachievement to personal empowerment. Provides national discipline and achievement statistics.

Enough is Enough: The Explosion in Los Angeles
[ISBN 1-880463-34-2] • $9.95

Provides an introspective analysis of the problems strangling those who live in America's urban battle zones and moves the reader toward solutions to help urban America help itself before it's tool late.

Fight-Free Schools: Creating a School Culture That Promotes Achievement
[ISBN 1-880463-14-8] • $29.95

Outlines all of the components and provides everything that a classroom teacher or principal needs to create a fight-free school environment: instructional lessons; charts; parent communication; letters to the community; classroom, cafeteria, school bus, and school-wide activities; a lesson on the human brain and what causes anger; sample newsletters; fight-free pledge cards; certificates, and more.

Follow Your Dreams: Lessons That I Learned in School
[ISBN 1-880463-51-2] • $7.95

All students are confronted with choices during their school-aged years, from kindergarten through college. Which group do I identify with? How seriously do I take my schoolwork? How important is it to establish goals? What are my dreams and aspirations? How can my time in school help me to achieve them?

Mychal Wynn shares his story about the lessons that he learned while grappling with such questions and how he became a high academic achiever along the road to discovering his dreams and aspirations.

Increasing Student Achievement: Volume I: Vision
[ISBN 1-880463-10-5] • $29.95

This, the first volume of the Increasing Student Achievement series, outlines how a school community goes about the business of developing a clearly-defined commonly shared vision that drives systemic and sustained efforts toward increasing student achievement.

Inspired to Learn: Why We Must Give Children Hope
[ISBN 1-880463-08-3] • $12.95

Stephen Peters, former middle school principal, not only outlines his vision for the children in our schools, he goes on to share how he and his staff turned their vision into operational strategies.

Ten Steps to Helping Your Child Succeed in School
[ISBN 1-880463-50-4] • $9.95

Outlines easy-to-follow steps for parents and teachers to better understand children so that we can better direct them. The steps help parents and teachers to easily identify a child's personality types, learning-styles, Multiple Intelligences, best and worst learning situations, dreams and aspirations.

Test of Faith: A Personal Testimony of God's Grace, Mercy, and Omnipotent Power [ISBN 1-880463-09-1] • $9.95

"This book has become more than a recalling of my hospital experiences, it has become a testimony of the power of the human spirit; a testimony of the healing power of the Holy Spirit; and ultimately a personal testimony of my relationship with God, my belief in His anointing, and my trust in His power, grace, and mercy."

The Eagles who Thought They were Chickens: A Tale of Discovery
Book • [ISBN 1-880463-12-1] • $4.95
Teacher's Guide • [ISBN 1-880463-18-0] • $9.95
Student Activity Book • [ISBN 1-880463-19-9] • $5.95

Chronicles the journey of a great eagle, historically perched at the right hand of the great king in her native Africa, who is captured and taken aboard a slave ship, the eggs that are eventually hatched, and their struggles in the chicken yard where they are scorned and ridiculed for their differences. The story offers parallels to behaviors in classrooms and on school playgrounds where children are teased by schoolyard "chickens" and bullied by schoolyard "roosters."

Visit our web site for a complete listing of our books,
materials, and training programs:

http://www.rspublishing.com
or call for a free catalog
(800) 524-2813

This Order May Be Placed By Mail • FAX • Telephone • E-mail
Payment May Be Made By Money Order • Check • Credit Card • Purchase Order

Enter the item number, description, corresponding price, and quantity for each selection (e.g., #5002, Don't Quit, $9.9 ea.) and compute the total for that item. Shipping is 10% of the subtotal, i.e., subtotal of $200.00 x .10 = $20.00 shippi charges). **Allow two weeks for processing.**

Item #	Description (Please Print)	Unit Price	X Quantity	= Total
5101	Empowering African-American Males	24.95		
5102	Empowering African-American Males Workbook	15.95		
6903	A High School Plan for Students with College-Bound ...	19.95		
6901	A Middle School Plan for Students with College-Bound ...	15.95		
7201	Ten Steps to Helping Your Child Succeed in School	9.95		
7901	Increasing Student Achievement: Volume I, Vision	29.95		
5601	The Eagles who Thought They were Chickens	4.95		
5602	The Eagles ... Student Activity Book	5.95		
5603	The Eagles ... Teacher's Guide	9.95		
5003	Follow Your Dreams: Lessons That I Learned in School	7.95		
5115	At-Risk Bundle *(23% savings)*	99.95		
	(Contains 5101, 5102, 6903, 6901, 7201, 7901, 5601, 5003)			

Method Of Payment
Do Not Send Cash • No C.O.D.s

❑ A check (payable to Rising Sun Publishing) is attached
o A purchase order is attached, P.O. # _____
Charge my:
❑ Visa ❑ Mastercard _____

Signature (required for credit card purchases) Expiration Date: _____

SUBTOTAL $_____

Shipping (Subtotal x .10) _____

Add Handling   **3.9**

Georgia residents

Add 6% Sales Tax _____

TOTAL: ___

✉ Mail to:
RISING SUN PUBLISHING
P.O. Box 70906
Marietta, GA 30007-0906

☎ Phone toll-free: **1.800.524.2813**
RISING SUN FAX: **1.770.587.0862**
PUBLISHING E-mail: orderdesk@rspublishing.com
Web site: http://www.rspublishing.com

Ship to *(Please Print)* [Must be same as billing address for credit card purchases]:
Name _____
Address_____
City_____ State _____ Zip _____
Day Phone (_____) _____ FAX: _____
E-mail Address: _____ Date: _____